BIG RIVER, BIG WOODS, BIG GAMES

Copyright 2013 by Joe Schwab
All rights reserved.

ISBN-10: 1482539411
EAN-13: 9781482539417

BIG RIVER, BIG WOODS, BIG GAMES

Joe Schwab

Forward

For the past several years I have been thinking about the first two books, mentally critiquing them, while watching them sell in the shops and stores along the Columbia River. I was searching ideas for a third book and in the process started several more writing stories and picking the ideas from other Wildlife Officer's experiences. I struggled to come up with something different while most of the people, friends, family, who read the books echoed the same words. They were left wanting more of the same!

Recently a friend of mine stopped by to visit and picked up both of the books. We had not seen each other for some time and he was eager to get into the tales. He later called me and told me how much he enjoyed them. He said his son began reading one of them and would not put it down until he finished it. And he said his son never reads books! These kinds of remarks encouraged me to get back to work writing. I tossed the new ideas and combined the stories I had written down into one last book.

The Columbia River flows by my front door on its unending journey to the Pacific Ocean. I can see the water surface from a few hundred yards away at high tide and I watch the ships as they make their way from the sea to Portland and back. On foggy mornings I awake to the mournful blast of the ship's horn as it slowly courses its way upriver rounding the curve at Goat Island and pointing its bow directly at my open window.

18 years have passed since I retired from Oregon State Police Fish and Wildlife. Every time I go to the river I recall another incident, another story, another place, another person. I wonder about all the twists and turns my life has taken and what would have happened had I taken another path. Would the stories have been different? I looked back on the first one and some reviews that followed. A common theme was, "It was too short." "The stories lacked detail." One former member suggested I delve into the recent history and workings of Wildlife Enforcement a little more that people really understand what "Wildlife Law" is (or was) all about.

So sit back in your favorite chair and enjoy the stories.

CHAPTER I
Here's how it all happened

I always had a love for the water going way back to my early childhood days dreaming and scheming ways to get my own boat and spend every waking moment on the water. This is part of the reason why I started my river career with the Wildlife Division of the Oregon State Police. The details are pretty much outlined in the first book so I won't repeat them.

Looking back on my first boating experience takes me all the way to a little lake in the outskirts of Minnesota called Pike Lake. After two and a half years of College, going nowhere, I joined the Air Force. I had just been transferred to Duluth Air Force Base by the U.S. Air Force in 1963 with a wife and three month old baby boy and no place to live. We arrived in Duluth on Labor Day weekend which fortunately turned out to be the best possible time. Rentals in town near the airbase were high priced but a kind gentleman told us of a resort on nearby Caribou Lake that closed its season after Labor Day and then rented cabins for the winter. That would give us time to find a suitable rental. We arrived at Caribou Lake, a beautiful little jewel just a few miles west of the airbase. The owners of the resort showed us what was available to rent and even offered the use of their boats for fishing.

My experience with boats to that point had been minimal; at best, so rowing would do just fine. I soon became proficient enough to venture several hundred yards offshore. Catching fish was the easy part and supplemented the family food budget. To make a long story short we managed through our first winter in Duluth and kept from freezing in -30 temperatures by sleeping on the floor of the living room on the mattress. We simply could not afford to heat the entire house. We had moved from the little cabin to an apartment and by summer we found a little house on Pike Lake nearby.

Tech Sergeant Joe Socha, my NCOIC who retired and now still lives in the area, had bought an old mahogany runabout with a 35 HP Gale motor. Being the kind man he always was, looking out for his Troops, he persuaded me to buy it from him for the grand sum of $125. Why I bought this boat still mystifies me? It was a piece of work and only the skill of my neighbor and best friend, Ray Campbell, made it operable. One day, fishing on Pike Lake by myself, I noticed a squall approaching. The motor refused to start and winds quickly reached plus 40 MPH on the lake kicking up whitecaps and waves. The only way I could make shore was toss the anchor and pull the rope, toss the anchor and pull the rope! It was a rough and exciting ride but just as I made it to shore the squall passed!

Ray and I spent many hours over the next several years catching Northern and Crappie. We would start fishing at dark and come in sometime after midnight prowling the lake mainly for Walleye. The plentiful Crappie kept us going back. We had no fish finders, but Ray was a fearless snorkler. He would swim ahead of the boat as I rowed, find the schools of fish and climb back in the boat to fish for them. Duluth Air Force Base and the surrounding area of lakes and woods was a great assignment and it seemed no one was ever transferred out so I reenlisted looking forward to more years of fishing the beautiful Northern lake country. Two months later in the fall of 1965 I was put on orders to Okinawa! The boat was passed on to another unsuspecting Airman before we left.

Once in Okinawa I began seriously planning my future career in Fish and Wildlife that had taken root many years before when I was 13. I read every publication I could get my hands on. During that time period, a conservation correspondence course ran ads in nearly every outdoor publication, proclaiming "Become a Game Warden, sleep under the stars and catch your breakfast from an icy brook!" It may have been hokey but it got my attention and kept the fire burning inside. In July of 1969 I received my second honorable discharge from the U.S. Air Force and came home to Oregon more determined than ever to join OSP and become a Wildlife Officer.

After preliminary job searches, filling out applications, physicals and background checks I finally received notice I would be hired by Oregon State Police on September 1, 1969. I was to report to the Police Academy at Camp Withycombe for 5 weeks of training followed by assignment to the Patrol Office at West Slope for further training. I was a bit apprehensive about more "basic training". After 8 years in the Air Force and advancement to Staff Sergeant I had a vague feeling I was starting all over; Nothing of the sort. We were greeted and treated like valued employees from day one. We handled the usual cleaning of the barracks and bedding but classroom and practical training took on a tone of "this is what you must learn to stay alive and keep the public safe." It was important enough to help each other through and build a lasting camaraderie with our classmates which remains to this day. In later years academy training took on more of a "recruit school" atmosphere leading to a more military style of training. Whether or not the style improved on the quality of the product is a matter of conjecture. All I know is that most of the members of our class and the ones before and immediately after advanced into very important positions within the Department. Few of them left unless it was for a much better job with another agency.

Police work requires that you rely upon and support your fellow Officers. They depend upon you and your life may well rest in their hands at any given moment. The five weeks flew by, we finished our class work, practical training and went off to our assignments ready to enter the world of Law Enforcement.

I had to wait for my opportunity to work my way into a Fish and Wildlife assignment. There were openings in the southern part of the State but we had already bought a house and were reluctant to relocate again. Patrol work was intriguing and would add to the overall experience. Many Wildlife Enforcement Officers enter into the assignment through the Patrol Division. It seems to be the one thing the public misunderstands the most about Oregon State Police Wildlife Enforcement. First and foremost all are State Troopers and are empowered and expected to enforce all State laws. Oregon and Alaska are the only two States organized in that manner and it seems to work very well. In many States, Wildlife Enforcement is considered an entry level job to higher positions. And unfortunately in many instances works accordingly.

We were assigned to coaches at our Stations for several months of on the job training, perhaps the most important training of a Police Officers career. The coaches were experienced Troopers guiding us through the fine points of safe stops, investigations, detections, report writing (of course) and safe high speed pursuit driving. Trooper John Tichenor, my coach for the duration of my training was fearless at pursuit driving. His control of a patrol car at speeds in excess of 80-90 MPH was uncanny and through his persistence, he raised my confidence and ability to handle high speed traffic encounters. I firmly believe to this day, the training has kept me accident free for over forty years and hundreds of thousands of miles driven; save for backing into a post once.

The patrol cars of that time were Plymouth 383s and Dodge 440s of the late 60s and early 70s. The speedometers went to 150 and so did the cars. Many chases on I-5, Hwy 26 and 99W went beyond 100 MPH. Traffic moved fast on the lighter traveled sections of new freeways often averaging 80+MPH. We had to patrol at speeds above 85 just to move with the traffic. Muscle cars dominated the freeways and adrenalin filled high speed chases seemed to be weekly occurrences in the Portland area.

Shortly after I finished my apprenticeship and was out on my own I was assigned I-5 patrol working between Wilsonville and Portland. One day I was passed by and paced a newer sedan at 125 MPH for a considerable distance and finally made the stop near Woodburn. The driver was an attorney and gave me little argument. I issued the citation and shortly received notice of trial in Salem.

I had never appeared before this Judge and as I gave my testimony he leaned forward as if doubting my statements. Usually the Defense would challenge our integrity, the accuracy of our speedometers, anything that would cast doubt on the testimony. This was not the case. The Attorney challenged none of my testimony. At the conclusion of my testimony the attorney moved for dismissal.

The Judge frowned and bellowed, "On what grounds?"

The attorney calmly argued that I had not proven a violation of the Basic Rule, which stated that speed alone, was not a factor in a violation. Other conditions had to exist.

The Judge became quite impatient and asked the attorney if he was indeed going 125. He replied that he probably was but felt that he did not violate the Basic Rule.

The Judge got became quite agitated and proceeded to chew the Attorney from top to bottom about driving at excessive speeds on "his" freeways. He quickly found the attorney guilty, fined him $500 and instructed me to issue a Reckless Driving citation if I ever caught this man again.

Patrolling I-5 in the Portland area to Wilsonville was seldom dull, especially around the holidays. One night, just before Christmas, I made my turn from I-5 onto Barbur Boulevard and was going south to re enter I-5 at Tigard. I noticed an object moving toward me in my lane and realized it was a northbound car in the southbound lanes with no lights; and moving fast! I turned into a parking lot to avoid the driver then took up chase. She drove less than 3 blocks before landing in a ditch and luckily suffered only bent fenders. But she somehow wanted to blame it on me on me and came out fighting! Based on her condition and the smell of alcohol I had no desire to waste time on sobriety tests and soon had her handcuffed in the back seat.

I radioed my location and mileage and headed for Rocky Butte Jail. It was a wet cold night about 2:30AM, the time Police Officers often referred to as the "magic hours", when all sorts of unexplained events occur, usually involving intoxicated drivers.

I turned from I-5 onto I 84 east and noticed taillights ahead, weaving from fog line to center line. I thought, "My god! Have the gates of DUII hell opened?" I was hoping maybe it was just a tired worker headed home, and called for another patrol. The dispatcher advised there were none available, as they were all busy with problems of their own. I flipped on the overhead lights and the weaving car slowly pulled over and stopped. As I was walking up to the door she stuck her head out questioning why I had stopped her. There was no doubt now. I asked her to step out and perform some sobriety checks. She nearly fell on the pavement and admitted to drinking, "too much".

Just as I finished putting her in the back seat, another car pulled up alongside my patrol car and a drunken slurred voice called out. "You need any help Officer!"

I moved over into the passenger window of the car and detected a strong odor of alcohol. My first inclination was to go around and remove the driver but I would have had to step into traffic, not a good option at that time of night. We managed to navigate the freeways in those days on foot as well as from patrol cars. It was common practice to dodge speeding cars while removing hazards from the roadway, a practice that would not even be attempted with today's volumes of traffic. This hazard had to be removed from the highway and the safest way seemed to be the most obvious.

"Yeah just pull it off the highway and I'll be right there." I said almost not believing what was happening that night. More tests, another tow truck and another client was in the front seat with me, all cuffed up and ready to go to jail. You see it just doesn't normally happen like this, but that night I was up to my neck in intoxicated drivers. The dispatcher by this time was most perplexed and kept asking if everything was alright. I assured her I was in control, though I wondered if I should just close my eyes to any further incidents that night. Fortunately there was plenty of manpower at the jail as I led my lineup of DUIIs thru the jailhouse doors.

At the hour of 4:00AM I returned to the Patrol Office and began several hours of report writing. In those days we typed with real manual typewriters, all reports in triplicate with carbon paper and no whiteout allowed!

Satisfaction washed over me later as I realized that just possibly, three more people lived to enjoy Christmas that year!

On December 6, 1970, a year later on night patrol south of Portland I received a call to assist Tim Mansfield a fellow Trooper and friend with a DUII. I saw Tim's patrol car ahead on the northbound shoulder north of Barbur Boulevard overpass. He was across the freeway in the southbound lanes with a stopped vehicle. In order to come in behind him I would have had to go several miles into Portland to turn around. I decided to just walk across the Freeway as it was late and traffic was almost non existent. Tim explained he had seen the motorist, who was now passed out in the front seat, driving slowly down the shoulder and stop just short of the Capitol Highway exit ramp. I walked up to the right side door and leaned in to check the driver. That was the last thing I remembered!

When I came to I was on a stretcher being carried to the Ambulance aided by probably a dozen Officers from Portland, Multnomah County, OSP, Washington County and Tigard PD. Flashing red blue and white lights added a surreal image to the scene as I tried to process what was happening. My head was buzzing and I was trying to make sense of what had happened. Did I wreck my car? Where was I? Why was I on a stretcher? Mike Plester, a burly Trooper holding one side of the stretcher, kindly admonished me for "eating too much chicken" as he struggled to hold up his corner of the stretcher.

Everything hurt including my head which had taken a blow from a car speeding down the shoulder of the highway intent on taking the exit ramp. Tim later described seeing the car coming and yelling at me to "jump". The car slammed into the one I was leaning into and threw me 20 to 30 feet up the embankment where I came to rest unconscious. Tim thought surely I was dead, broadcasting for immediate assistance. Doctor James Schimschok, Emmanuel Hospital Physician, checked me over and after a one night stay in the hospital, and 3 days recovering at home I was cleared to go back to work on December 9. Coincidentally he was our family Doctor while serving as a Captain in the U.S. Air Force at Duluth AFB several years prior.

Our old District Captain had come out to the scene and later on told the story many times over about how I woke up and the first thing I asked about was my patrol car. He would laugh about it but any young Trooper could tell horror stories about repercussions from damaged patrol cars.

For months afterward I would get flashbacks while standing on the pavement when the noises reached a certain crescendo. The hair would stand up on the back of my neck and my senses would heighten. Once it was brought to a head when I was writing a citation to a speeding motorist and looking back at approaching traffic, I noticed an 18 wheeler slowly veering toward me standing just inside the fog line. I sensed I had to bail out and reached inside the open window of the motorists car, grabbed the inside of the windshield and jumped up on the hood of the car just as the duals of the semi passed over the fog line where I had been standing. I tossed the license back to the driver, told him to forget the citation and fell into pursuit of the truck. It didn't take more than a mile to haul the truck driver over and stride up to the door ready for a confrontation. The driver was scared and apologizing, realizing what he had done. My first inclination was to haul him out physically and administer a little street justice. Neither of us would have benefited and with his assurance that he would watch more closely when passing a Trooper engaged in a stop he was sent on his way. Now the move over law has been put into effect ending or at least decreasing the risk to Troopers on potentially life threatening traffic stops.

I found the old Officers Report with Superintendent Holly Holcomb's initials on it, describing the incident. Superintendent Holcomb was killed by an assassin in front of Headquarters several years later.

Many Troopers across the country have paid the ultimate price due to inattentive or intoxicated drivers clipping them at high speeds. Trooper Dan Nelson fell in a similar accident on I-5 two years later. I have reflected back on that night many times and wondered what it was that saved me.

I put some experiences into verse.

One cold night, December 23 as I recall, while working graveyard.
I had just made turn back south on Barbur Boulevard
heading down from Capitol Highway cresting the hump
When I saw something heading my way, in my lane!

I was caught by the motion,
headed the big patrol car to the shoulder,
as the unlighted car passed, speeding,
oblivious to anything in her path.

She ended up in the ditch unhurt after a hard right
and unfazed by my now flashing overhead light.
She greeted me with a string of profanity
as if I had caused her troubles, insanity!

It was too easy, her sobriety check failed,
She bought her one way ticket to Rocky Butte Jail
I radioed the dispatch center and headed north on I-5,
My cargo secure in cuffs and seatbelt in the back seat, alive.

I took the exit off I-5 onto 84 E
I saw brake lights flashing in front of me.
A car was driving slowly in the right lane
weaving from fog line to center line.

"Damn, is there no end to this madness!" I thought to myself.
I called in to see if there was an extra patrol in town.
"Nope, all of them were busy this cold winter night
with plenty of problems of their own."

*I flipped on the overhead lights, hoping
this was just a tired worker the way home.
She pulled off on the shoulder of I 84
I slowly approached her driver door.*

*"What's the problem Officer?" she cried out the window.
My instincts told me it was going to be a long night.
Quick tests confirmed my suspicions
and another passenger placed in the back.*

*As I walked back to my door, a car stopped alongside!
"Hey Officer! Do ya need some help?" a slurred voice called out.
By now I was wondering if the gates of "DUI hell" were ajar.
I said, "Sure friend, pull over in front of me and get off the tar."*

*I went through the steps of the testing once more
He complied and joined me in the front seat of my patrol car.
I was getting intoxicated by the smell of alcohol inside.
Tow trucks arrived and swiftly took the cars away into the night.*

*The dispatcher, by this time was just a little bemused
And my situation had him a little confused
I calmly assured him that all was well,
and I would be enroute to the Graybar Hotel.*

*The rest was easy. I headed to the Jail,
dropped off my passengers, knowing they'd post bail..
I was a little numb from events of that day.
It usually doesn't happen that way.*

*I looked at my watch, 3:40 AM, put on my belt, made sure it was tight,
I had a strange feeling. a perverse sort of triumph that night.*

*Three people were jailed for too many beers,
and would undoubtedly be out for the next evening cheer.
But maybe, just maybe they and some others
lived to enjoy the Holiday that year!*

Merry Christmas!

Author and his patrol car, 1969 Plymouth Fury 383. The old Sam Browne leather, breeches and boots. The uniform of the day.

Another night, Trooper Tony Marshall called out on his radio that a driver had deliberately tried to hit him near the Zoo. We all headed that way to intercept the now fleeing car. Trooper John Grosz and I were closest and near Cedar Hills and Hwy 26 we fell in behind. Rolling road blocks had been used before with some success so we set up the plan. At speeds of near 80MPH it had to be done right the first time.

I accelerated and passed Tony and the violator to get the lead position. John came in alongside as I slowed to block the car. The way it usually worked was with a patrol car behind, alongside and in front, the violator would be forced onto the shoulder and stopped with no where to go. I was watching closely in my rear view mirror when suddenly the violator accelerated trying to ram me from behind. Fortunately I had more power and was able to outrun him but hit close to 100MPH doing so. My choices were limited so I took the exit at 185th and went up then back down onto Highway 26 and fell in behind. We needed another plan. It became obvious the driver was not going to stop and someone was going to get hurt.

A Washington County Deputy entered the chase near North Plains. He decided to end the chase by ramming the fleeing car. This was an option that was not available to OSP at the time. Fortunately it worked and the car spun out into the soft grassy median. He was trying to get back onto the highway as I used my push bars to shove him back into the dirt ending the chase.

Only then did we realize that the fleeing motorist had his wife and child in the car with him. He was raving, swearing and threatening us as we surrounded the car. He had locked the doors but neglected to lock the old style wind wing. I shoved my hand in through the open wing and grabbed his long hair. As I pulled his head forward another Officer reached in and unlocked the door. It took three of us to remove him from the car and handcuff him. All the while his wife was screaming at us for "endangering" their lives. I think she had things just a little mixed up.

He was taken to jail for Driving under the influence and Reckless driving.

What is a State Trooper?

Decked out in blue with his campaign hat and spit shined leather He moves out into the night, fearing nothing. He is prepared, and confident.

Whatever comes his way, he meets with a professional gaze, utters just the right words and calms situations that panic mere mortals.

Little children, frightened by loss of contact with their parents, wrap their tiny arms around his broad shoulders and bury their heads, somehow knowing the Trooper will make things better. If at all possible he will.

He understands the crushing feeling of a lost loved one. He has seen it too often. But many times the words just won't come. And his only reply is "I'm sorry!"

He stands between evil and innocence, never shirking from his duty in the face of danger.
He and the Troopers he works with and relies upon have formed a bond.

It is a bond that lasts forever, even when age and retirement force Troopers to yield to youth.
A feeling of pride washes over the "old guys" when those who follow, uphold the honor they have helped create.

You never stop being a "Trooper"

BIG RIVER, BIG WOODS, BIG GAMES

Oregon State Police Honor Guard at the groundbreaking of the Fallen Trooper Memorial ceremony.

CHAPTER II
Working the river

After a few short and exciting years working patrol I landed my Wildlife position. This was what I had come for and this was the path I was going to follow.

I was soon assigned to Commercial Fish Enforcement on the Columbia River. My first patrol boat was a sea worthy 21 foot Seabird. I would patrol the areas around Portland from Bonneville Dam to Sauvie Island with anyone who would accompany me. Few had the interest for the river that I had, preferring to work the surrounding mountains and forests instead. My strong desire to work the Big River landed me at St. Helens at the same time the Department took delivery a brand new 1973 19 foot Fiberform Hardtop Cuddy with Decca Radar. The boat was the pride of the fleet, outclassed only by its big brother a 24 foot Fiberform, same color, same configuration stationed at Astoria.

Hank and I drove to Portland and picked up the boat then headed back to St. Helens on a familiarization cruise. Everything worked. The radar was a huge benefit to working the often foggy lower Columbia River. On foggy night patrols we would put the hood on the radar screen so only one person could see it. The boat operator would try to steer a predetermined course using only the compass and fairly primitive depth finder. This quickly enhanced our skills thus navigating the river at night became easier and safer.

Ninety percent of the time we operated without lights of any kind. The boat was equipped with high intensity spotlights and creeping up on violators and lighting them up was always a rousing state of affairs. Only the most "experienced" poachers would have the presence of mind to run. Wild chases in the middle of the night, spotlights cutting a path in the darkness, wakes left by the fleeing outlaws, and radios blaring directions of travel to other patrol boats, when there was backup, added to the seemingly chaotic scenes. Adrenalin ran high and recounting the chases, much like evaluating high speed car chases, left us feeling fortunate and sometimes just plain lucky to have avoided equipment damage or worse.

I don't recall any injuries suffered by any of the Officers that worked the river, other than a sudden soaking in 40 degree water or a skinned knee from a fall during a foot chase. We had to be extremely careful boarding commercial boats both in the river and at sea. While most of the commercial operators knew we were coming aboard and never made any dangerous moves, there were a few Captains who "accidentally" turned the wheel or hit the throttle at that critical point of jumping the deck. It was a stupid thing to do and usually resulted in very thorough inspections that consequently earned them a citation into court.

Some nights during the Early Winter gill net seasons on the River, the temperature would drop below freezing. The decks of the boats became sheet ice. Boarding was hazardous at best and skippers were not being cooperative. They did not like being boarded and would simply ignore our attempts and continue on despite being hailed and ordered to stand by. On those kinds of nights it was best to just call it off and go home, risk not being worth the reward.

In the mid 70s the Coast Guard joined enforcement with State Officers especially on the offshore fishery. They took an entirely different and much more serious attitude about skippers who tried to refuse boarding. National Marine Fisheries Service also provided assistance to the States in the form of equipment and money to lease larger boats for longer patrols. It was a pleasure to stand at the wheel of the 52 foot Corliss, owned by Washington Department of Fisheries and operated by Captain Dan O'Hagen. This boat was no comparison to the barely adequate boats we worked with. The vessel was big, fast and very seaworthy. One of its assets was the 15 foot Zodiac racked on the deck. We cruised far offshore out of sight of the fishing fleets, launched the Zodiac over the side, suited up and headed for the large concentrations of commercial and sport fishing boats.

We hid in the swells keeping out of sight until we were in the middle of the fleet. Quickly noting the gear on each boat, suspect boats were identified, and boarded. In one instance, a boat with three fishermen on board had commercial downriggers deployed but no commercial fishing license displayed. They had 37 lures total still in the water fishing when we boarded them! They were just a bunch of sport fishermen who shrugged begrudgingly and accepted their tickets.

The most distasteful job to me was boarding commercial trollers and inspecting the holds below decks. Fish holds were smelly, slimy with not a hint of fresh air. The rocking and rolling seas contributed to the sense of "mal de mer" the dreaded seasickness! I was susceptible to the condition and no amount of Dramamine or lemon drops would stop it. Taking the wheel was the only way to avoid getting sick. Later after retirement I ran my own charter boat fishing for salmon and halibut in Alaska and never got sea sick but I had great compassion for my clients who did.

1975 Fiberform Hardtop Cuddy Cabin. Our new patrol boat snug in its moorage. The boat was seaworthy and comfortable for the long night patrols.

Beaching the boat

A "new" 24 foot Duckworth Magnum had been seized from a drug dealer and turned over to us for river use. I was operating at a pretty high speed downriver from Clatskanie on a kind of shakedown cruise to see what the boat was capable of. The 460 cubic inch engine with jet pump operated flawlessly, until something came loose! There was a loud bang and the boat started vibrating badly throwing water inside the engine housing. I pulled the engine cover and discovered a section of the pump had broken and was spewing more water inside the boat than out thru the jet drive. The bilge pumps could not keep up with the flow and of course the engine had lost all power. We had to get to shore quickly or sink in the 40 foot deep channel. Fortunately we had a 10 HP kicker motor we quickly started and headed the boat to shore. We hit shallow water nosing it onto a small stretch of beach. We had to get it towed before the tide went out and left us high and dry. I called dispatch to explain our problem and told them to send a boat from Astoria to assist us. Norm was on the water downriver and responded in less than an hour. By the time he arrived we were indeed high and dry. He surveyed the situation and came ashore to discuss how we could pull the grounded boat to deeper water and tow it back to the ramp. We patched the hole with plastic and duct tape well enough to survive a slow tow. Norm took several pictures of the boat and I suspected what he was going to do with them.

With shovels and two by fours we moved the bow around to an angle pointing toward the water and secured a heavy tow line. The big jet boat got in as close as possible and began pulling. The rush of water from the jet pump was blowing the sand away from the bottom of the grounded boat easing the removal. Slowly the grounded boat moved toward the water and after some pushing and pulling it was afloat again. Norm towed us back upriver to our trailer, where we loaded up and left for the repair shop.

As one of the Supervisors, I had counseled Officers on grounding and boat damage incidents over the years. At our yearly Wildlife School later they proudly presented me with the "Sandbar Sailor" award including pictures of the beached craft. I protested I had saved a boat from sinking but it was payback none the less. And who could blame them?

I got the last laugh on Norm when we later acquired a 24 foot Hurricane rigid hull inflatable boat equipped with the latest gear and two large engines. It was assigned to Astoria for patrolling the dangerous bar and ocean waters.

Norm and another Officer took it out on a familiarization cruise and while outside the bar, one of the engines lost power. Norm was unable to determine what went wrong as the engine would not lift up and seas were rough so he decided to take it in to the Coast Guard Station at Cape Disappointment. The one engine capably brought them in and as they docked, one of the Coasties walked up to the boat.

After a quick assessment he commented with a grin, "Gee It looks like you have a crab pot rope tangled on your starboard engine. That's probably why you lost power?"

It was still attached to the crab pot! It was quickly removed and never mentioned to anyone. But somehow I found out.

I sport fish at a local beach regularly now that I'm retired and one morning just a few years ago I got there a little late as usual. One of the regulars came running up to me and said, "You just missed it!"

"What did I miss?" I asked, eager to hear perhaps another story.

"The Staters were just here and pulled their boat into the beach to check us out," One of them exclaimed, "and then they almost lost their boat! Here let me show you on my video."

The video captured the boat slowly backing away from the beach as one of the Troopers watched helplessly. The fishermen were laughing while one of them explained the situation.

The Troopers pulled onto the beach and left the boat running as they checked licenses. The operator apparently thought he had put it in neutral but actually left it in reverse. Jet pumps take awhile to respond when idling and when the last Trooper got off, the boat slowly backed into deeper water. All the Trooper could do was stand there and watch his boat backing away from the beach. Just when it looked hopeless the boat slowly turned around and began backing toward the beach once again. I can only imagine the thoughts of the Trooper watching a $100,000 boat moving without a pilot. As it backed closer to shore he was able to jump aboard and assume control.

I watched the video several times, laughing to myself, and then asked the fisherman if I could forward a copy to Jeff the Sergeant at Astoria. Jeff, one of the former recipients of the Sandbar Sailor award thanked me and assured me he would put the video to good use later.

Patrolling the estuary and the Pacific Ocean in the Zodiac. Though small these were extremely seaworthy boats and when coupled with the 52 foot Corliss, gave us the flexibility needed to extend patrols.

CHAPTER III
Fishing at the Estuary

In the early 1970s the salmon fishery was much different offshore and in the Columbia River than it is today. There was no such thing as a fin clip or differentiation between hatchery and wild fish. There were simply "Chinook" and "Coho", with occasional Pinks thrown in. On busy weekends I would run the patrol boat to 60 miles to Astoria and spend the weekend outside checking sport boats with one of the Troopers from Astoria.

Hard boats, as we referred to fiberglass and wooden boats of the era ran out of Hammond, Astoria, Ilwaco, Chinook and every other small harbor in the area to the rich feeding grounds just off the Columbia River mouth. We usually waited until the sport boats were well into the morning fishery and had fish on board. We would head out and pick a boat to board and inspect catches. We had only a few rules to enforce, Salmon size, over limits, tagging violations and number of rods and hooks.

On a good day we would find a half dozen or more extra illegal "meat lines", ingenious devices, clipped to the tow hooks, sea anchors, dock lines or just hanging over the side of the boat. Heavy monofilament with bungee cords to absorb the shock of a fish hitting the line was the usual.

"Extra fish" were stashed in cabins under the cushions, under floorboards, in fake gas cans with bottoms that opened up, or fish boxes with false bottoms. I'm sure there were many more hidden holes we never found. The human mind is capable of finding extremely clever ways of hiding illegal fish and game. Just when you think you have seen it all, you see something new.

Jumping boats was a fine art as well as a dangerous one. I often wish we had used video cameras to document the happenings. When we decided to board a boat, the conditions were carefully considered. We lined up the approach and the boarding Officer positioned himself on the Starboard side. Our operator would run alongside at a speed just slightly faster than the fishing boat. We would usually tell the boat to keep trolling as the seas would toss the boats haphazardly when they were put in neutral. At the last second the patrol boat would gently close the gap to a foot or less and the boarding Officer would step over into the other boat as the patrol boat operator hit the throttle and turned away. The same procedure was used when retrieving the Officer to the patrol boat. The Coast Guard did not like the procedure and let us know frequently. They considered it a hazardous practice but there really was no other way to get it done. Once we began using Zodiac inflatable boats boarding became much safer for everyone. The inflatable hulls allowed the boat operator to nose up against the hard boats and the boarding Officer could safely step onboard.

Inflatables were not completely soft though. On one patrol with the Coast Guard offshore near Tillamook I was performing boarding duties along with the Coast Guard crew. The seas were running high, almost to the point of cancellation, but we wanted to get in a few more boats inspections on the commercial fleet. The Avon inflatable was lowered over the side of the 87 foot Coastal Patrol Vessel. I was the last one to board the inflatable and was hanging over the side on the rope ladder when the larger Vessel rolled toward me leaving me swinging out over the water still some 6 feet above the inflatable. The Chief on Deck yelled at me to drop as the Vessel was rolling back. If I hung on I would slam into the steel plating on the side. I let go and dropped onto the center console hitting on the small of my back. It hurt like hell but we had to get away from the bigger boat. The cox hit the throttle as I rolled to the floor in pain. After we finished the patrol I went to the quarters for a hot shower to relieve the pain. The next day we were back on the water but my back was never the same.

Most of the offshore violations consisted of illegal gear, protected species on board or licensing violations. When crab seasons ended there were usually high numbers of commercial crab pots left in the ocean. Owners were contacted and cited. Inspections of commercial fish buying stations produced illegal species or exceeding poundage quotas. The work required a keen knowledge of types and species of ground fish and the ability to cover large areas unannounced. Complicated rules, seasons and quotas often left Officers and fishermen confused.

Big off shore commercial boats operate today with GPS tracking systems and closed circuit cameras monitoring deck activities. Computers allow Officers to simply log on and observe but the old tactics are still used.

Developing cases

While patrols were the mainstay of the Commercial Fish Enforcement Officers, it was common practice to sit and observe, sometimes for hours and sometimes for days before developing enough information to make cases. On going fisheries such as the Tribal fisheries in the Upper River required case building information. Simply catching a couple of fishermen with a load of fish was futile and time consuming for the paltry sentences the Judges handed down. In the late 1970s, Officers began to question the lengthy seasons the Departments were authorizing for 50-100 Ceremonial fish. They knew through experience and pulling illegal nets that were left overnight, that it was not unusual to catch 25 fish in one net in one night.

Several of the permits, for instance, authorized the use of 5 nets for 5 nights for 50 fish! Managers simply did not believe or realize the system was being abused. If the fishermen were checked after the first night they would feign surprise at the large amounts of fish they had taken and turn them over to the tribe for ceremonial use. When they were not checked they reported being unsuccessful and disposed of the fish through illegal channels. Things were not adding up and it was decided to set up surveillance on the nets sites and the off loading sites.

Officers went to surveillance positions, armed with cameras, night vision gear, notebooks and recorders. They were documenting numbers of fish caught, kinds of fish caught, when they were caught, who caught them and the times they were offloaded. Rules required a tribal representative be present to take possession of the fish each day. The fish were not allowed to be transported or stored in any commercial facility or anywhere that was not noted on the permit.

Several years earlier another Officer and I came across 15 Ceremonial Salmon being delivered to a wholesale fish dealer in

Rainier in total violation of the permit. All parties were cited and convicted in court. Other instances involved Traffic Patrol Officers stopping Tribal members transporting Salmon into Portland in the wee hours of the morning, all in violation of permit rules. Numerous restaurants and fish markets were cited in the Portland area after being checked and found with undocumented gill net caught salmon on the premises. Some could have come from illegal lower river gillnets but the information told us they likely came from the upriver fishery.

Officers on surveillance began comparing notes with the Tribal representatives, all the while avoiding giving away any of their surveillance information. They found their information closely matched with the types and numbers of fish being reported with the exception of the fish that were not accounted for. After working, watching and documenting for weeks during the Spring Season the Officers were ready to file charges. One permit had exceeded its 50 fish allocation by over 300 fish! Others permits were exceeded by hundreds more. Tribal Elders voiced their concern and embarrassment at the handling and illegal disposal of Ceremonial caught fish.

Previously when large numbers of illegal fish had been seized from unattended nets the State had offered these fish to the tribes to use for their ceremonies. The tribes turned the offer down, claiming ceremonial fish were sacred fish that could only be handled by specified tribal members. (You know, the same tribal members who had been selling those sacred fish!) Now that it came to light that those specified members were abusing the privilege of gathering fish for the tribes and possibly even selling them! I attended one meeting with my Commanding Officer at the reservation to discuss the problems. One particularly obnoxious Tribal member made it very clear that we were there only at their invitation and our uniforms and badges meant nothing to them. I wanted to get up and leave but the meeting had to take place.

The Tribal leaders voiced concern that a certain criminal element on the river had taken over and it was up to the States of Oregon and Washington to deal with it. They expressed concern that their law abiding members could not fish or even sell their own fish without going through the "mafia" as they referred to the purveyors of illegal fish. We left them with the assurance we would put forth all effort we could to deal with the problem. I had my doubts that we had the manpower or the means to accomplish much more than we had already done.

NMFS in the meantime was gearing up with their undercover operation. "Salmon Scam" was born! The operation has been discussed and rehashed many times even in my first book, "Oulaws on the Big River" so there is little need in going over it again. It consisted of a multi State, multi Agency operation of overt, covert and deep undercover operations that lasted over one year. When it was over hundreds of citations were written and dozens of trials in State and Federal Courts were held. Suffice it to say there were few Not Guilty verdicts.

Wayne Lewis, a former OSP Wildlife Officer, who served as Director of Enforcement for NMFS during this operation is the Author of "Sea Cop" a finely detailed chronology of several large cases offshore and especially the one that became known as "Salmon Scam."

Many of the illegal players in the operation improved their lives for the better after it was all over. Of course not all the fishermen were outlaws and those who were not stayed on the sidelines watching the operation play out. On nights when things were quiet I often wandered down and old road that accessed the river just below Cascade Locks. A small parking area that could hold only a couple cars led to a trail that ended at an old fishing scaffold. If I was lucky Percy Brigham would be there sitting in the dark tending his dip net or hoop net.

He would say, "Hi Schwab, how you doing tonight?" in the soft monotone voice of his.

I always felt welcome to sit and listen to his stories. He had the age lines in his face of an old Native American that had seen and done it all. His long salt and pepper grey hair hung to his shoulders. He spoke in a wonderful clipped style of speech of days gone by when he was younger and fished over the churning rapids of the untamed Columbia.

"I remember," he would say, "I could fish where I wanted on the river. Old Tony, the Fish Cop watched me like I was a poacher."

Then he would laugh, "Tony was a good man though. Sorta' like you." He nodded laughingly.

I didn't quite know how to take him. But I really liked the old man. I wished I could have been there before the dams. Sorta'!

I heard many stories about Tony Krivack, the old Trooper Fish Cop who braved the river in tiny boats by himself, ski patrolled the slopes of Mt. Hood well into his eighties, retired from the Navy before he joined the State Police and was a true folk legend in the area.

Percy had little use for the modern methods of fast boats and run and gun techniques used by the younger tribal fishermen. He had a grudging respect for those of us in uniform that had a job to do. He understood why we enforced the laws that our government had placed on the Tribal fishery even though he did not agree with them. On occasion he would drop hints that certain people in certain places at times were abusing the regulations. Many of the regulations were there to protect what little was left and he did not tolerate abuses of the fishery from anyone. We respected him enough to never disclose the source of our information if we were able to act on it.

I wish now I had kept a small recorder to document his words as only he could speak them. There were other old timers in the commercial and sport fisheries on the river who shared their stories with me. But there were none the likes of Percy.

Bonneville Power Administration, eager to do what they could to enhance the declining fish runs, provided money for equipment that the States could never afford. Even with new equipment, extra positions and money for overtime it felt like a losing battle.

Keeping Wildlife Officers interest in a declining fishery where activities were slow was challenging. Most of them preferred to work elsewhere and at least contact people on occasion. BPA funded positions specifically for the River just to keep a presence. Finally in 1995 the runs showed an increase and allowed fishing once again on the Columbia. By that time I had retired and moved to Alaska.

When fishing runs, are low, violations usually decrease, although their impact is higher. Once the runs increase the violation rates increase and the entire cycle begins again. I've been asked numerous times what the driving force behind wildlife crimes is. Is it greed, opportunity, mistake, gathering instinct, competition, payback (that one always puzzled me) or just plain wildlife vandalism?

Oddly enough I received a book for Christmas this year, a journal written by Washington Irving. It described his travels on the plains of Arkansas and Oklahoma while the Army was trying to round up errant Plains tribes and move them to reservations. What struck me was, throughout the book, he described the wanton killing and waste of wildlife, Deer, Elk, Buffalo and Turkeys shot by roaming soldiers with no thought to limits or need. They were simply dumped at the fires and roasted, feasting on them till they were satisfied then left for the Buzzards as they moved on. I related this to modern problems, thrill killing, wasting and exceeding. While there were no laws governing wildlife there were certainly sensibilities that must have been considered. Poaching is not a modern problem by any stretch of the imagination. Man has only been limited by the weapons he possessed and was proficient with.

No creature on this earth kills strictly for the pleasure of killing besides man. I've heard the stories of Wolf packs laying waste to entire herds of animals. I don't believe for one minute though that it is a conscious decision with no intent to use the kill. Left to its own, the predator will kill and return to feed until it is gone. Other predators may run them off and claim the kill for their own or humans may interfere.

Many retired Wildlife Officers give up the sport of hunting, unwilling to participate in the activity because of the abuses they have witnessed over the years. Others pursue it with a passion as they see the need to contribute to the rich heritage that has existed for hundreds, perhaps thousands of years.

The longer I have been retired, the more stories I encounter of past and present abuses of the rules. Several organizations have been formed to work toward the enhancement of wildlife and assist enforcement of the laws through reward programs.

Plentiful fish runs, especially along the areas where commercial fishing occurred, seemed to bring out the "predators". And unlike crimes involving wildlife, there was another factor in crimes involving fish; profit! The ease of selling illegal fish was too tempting. Nearly all the isolated docks on the lower Columbia River had piles of old nets lying around. We paid close attention to these "rags" and took note when they were moved or seemed extremely wet with fresh vegetation in the webbing. A sure sign they had been soaked recently.

Information was hard to come by and plain old hard work seldom produced the results some Supervisors wanted to see. A few of the older more hardened Supervisors who had their share of time in the field understood the game. Most of the time, numbers of arrests was not a sign of prevention. They were a sign of high rates of violations, and wildlife could not sustain high rates of violations along with healthy hunting and fishing opportunity for the lawful users.

I recently read an article by a noted scientist who claimed that the only limiting factor to the loss of fish runs prior to the coming of the White man was the limited populations of the tribes that inhabited the Columbia Basin and its tributaries. They simply could not harvest all the fish that entered the system with their primitive methods. I tend to consider that theory as a little too simplistic. Harvest, even after the appearance of the white man on the scene was only limited by the ability to preserve and dispose through trade or sales.

I was giving a talk and doing a book signing one night to a group of Oregon Hunters Association members. After the talk an old friend who had retired long before I did and had risen to Command Staff at General Headquarters confided in me that the Staff often wondered what we did out there on the river on those lonely fruitless nights. They wondered if in fact we were performing productive work or just chasing boats. I think he went away with a little more appreciation of what the job was all about. It had little to do with the productivity of writing citations but more about preventing the wholesale losses of perhaps hundreds of thousands of valuable fish. There was no doubt our presence on the river was known and talked about by the fishing crowds. Quantifying that on paper was difficult. Paperwork though drove police work. Statistics, numbers, whatever one wanted to call it, we felt we were a necessary part of the entire scheme. I am convinced now more than ever having been able to verify the scope of violations that occurred on the river years later, that we had an important impact, yet we could have done more had the emphasis been prioritized.

Years later, I've been able to talk with Tug Boat operators, even retired Commercial Fishermen and Sport fishermen who have confirmed many suspicions we had. Literally hundreds of undersize Sturgeon, unwanted Steelhead or illegal wild ESA fish have been dumped on the passing decks of Tugboats or taken to shore and dropped off during the legal seasons. Paid Observers, stationed on Commercial boats during legal seasons, observed violations of rules regarding tanglenet operation procedures but were told to mind their own business and just count fish as they were instructed.

One of the old Administrators, talking about illegal fishing at night compared it to robbing a bank with little or no penalty attached. Many of us working the river compared fishing at night to walking into a bank, taking out money, filling out our own deposit slip and leaving. Don't get me wrong. Many if not most of the gill netters were honest hard working men and would not steal a pencil from the office. But later in my career, to put things in perspective, I put in some time at the Oregon Lottery. Winning tickets, mailed in, had to be opened in the presence of at least two officials and under the scrutiny of a closed circuit camera. Money in casinos was never handled by less than two people. No one was trusted to be alone with thousands of dollars in cash. Yet hundreds of thousands of dollars worth of publicly owned fish were handled at night by one person with nothing more than a slip of paper as proof of the catch. Add this to the fact that mishandling thousands of dollars worth of fresh fish at night during closed seasons often brought only a $500 fine. Finally, after years of abuse and outright thievery of the resource, the legislature saw the obvious and made it a Felony but only if it exceeded a set amount of value.

One night unable to sleep I penned some verse to describe the actions and mindset that I thought drove these poachers to their deeds.

Outlaw and the Tree

Mighty men, they boast of themselves,
Born to conquer, raised to steal.
The shadowed Cottonwoods hide their moves
And the wind in the leaves quiet their deals.

For those who long for backwater life,
The Outlaw existence calls some forth
Nature remains the last resort
And seldom complains, never retorts

Then finally comes the reckoning day
The bounty ceases, the Earth gives no more.
The Outlaw has taken all there is.
He's most surely rotted clear to the core.

He looks to the skies and shakes his fist.
Is that all there is? What have I missed?
He realized he failed to repay what he stole.
And has nothing to show for it now that he's old.

As he lies on the moist earth and breathes his last sigh.
He's taken by that which he never let by.
Time passes on as the earth claims its fee.
And where he lay dying, there now sprouts a tree.

A tree that nurtures, protects and secures.
And give shelter to God's least creatures.
Who would have dreamt it, why was it so?
The Outlaw would in the end cause it to grow

One of the old decaying fish stations at Mayger, no longer in use, has recently fallen into the river destroyed by a passing ship wake. It is symbolic of the changing times on the river.

CHAPTER IV
The River and the Cases

Another story was related to me by an anonymous source. He agreed to allow me to tell the story in his words.

A small slough that ran off the main river supported several boathouses. People lived and raised their families there off the bounty that the hills and river provided. Some did it legally; others did it whenever they felt they needed it. "It" in most cases consisted of harvesting the Salmon runs that came up the river from late winter to late fall.

The river was a big dark hole at night and even the sound of a small outboard was swallowed up by the immensity of the system. An hour of two before daylight they would retrieve the net and fish, load them into the boat and escape up the channel to their home, undetected even by their neighbors. All anyone ever knew was that more fish were available to buy or barter. Few cared or even bothered to ask where the fish came from.

On one particular night though, a heavy mist covered the surface of the river. Landmarks were still visible but nothing on the surface of the water was, not even the patrol boat as it idled along the abandoned rows of piling that had once held an old cannery. The tide was slack so there was no danger of current pushing the larger boat into the pilings. Easing back and forth on the throttle I bumped along looking into the blackness as my partner scanned with night vision gear. Brett saw line coming off the piling and stretching tightly into the black water. He reached out with the boat hook and pulled on the line.

"I think we got one!" he smiled. "It feels heavy and something is moving in it."

We checked to be sure it was a set net and that had been recently set, then backed off. We had no idea where the people who set the net were or if they had seen us, but we had time to wait.

Along about 3:00AM we heard the sound of a small outboard motor break the silence. As it became louder we could tell it was coming from the side channel that entered the river just above us. Adrenalin begins to build as the expected confrontation gets near. We couldn't see anything with the naked eye but with the night vision optics movement was seen as the boat cleared the weeds and grass at the entrance to the slough and headed our way.

Anticipating the violators coming to our location we were preparing to confront them when we realized they were not coming across but heading upriver. We had the shadows in our favor but were a bit undecided at what we should do. Letting the boat get out of sight could mean no case. We could hear the muffled voices of the men in the boat and it was obvious they had not seen us. Hopefully the sound of their motor would drown out the sound of our starter as we fired up and started to follow in their faint wake.

This is decision making time. Should we back off a known illegal net to follow a boat up the river in the darkness, not knowing for sure if it is the boat that will come back to the net or perhaps just an early sport fisherman heading out to his spot on the river? Many times in the past we had come across fishermen sitting in their boats waiting for the daylight to arrive.

This time it was different. The boat did not continue out into the river but slowed then stopped at another row of old pilings off the main channel. We cut the power and drifted still in the shadows of the mountains behind us blotting our outline. Now with the night vision trained on the figures in the boat it became obvious what they were up to. A boat hook reached into the water alongside a piling and came up with a line attached to several floats. As the floats and attached net came up out of the water we could hear the slapping of fish as they hit the sides and bottom of the small aluminum boat. Two, three, fat Springers hit the floorboards of the boat and were given a whack that crossed their eyes and terminated their flopping.

Now it was just a matter of a safe apprehension. We waited till they started their engine and headed back our way before we moved to block their escape. The powerful spotlight lit them up and temporarily blinded them. Unable to see anything they tried to race one way, then the other bumping off pilings and running into shallow water.

"OK guys, shut it down", Brett ordered! "State Police, Fish and Game!"

At first the two looked like deer caught in the headlights, eyes squinting, looking for a hole to run to. We were watching for any further movement on their part and at the same time looking for anything they might consider using as a weapon. They shut down and meekly surrendered, unlike some of the previous poachers we had encountered, who had responded by racing off into the dark, tossing evidence overboard and even trying to ram the patrol boat.

"You two climb aboard, and behave yourselves." Brett said, as they handed him the line from their skiff.

They were a couple of teenagers, suited up in ratty raingear and smelling like they had just cleaned the stable. I turned the patrol boat and headed back to the first net. We coasted in to the piling and grabbed the line that was attached to the other gillnet. As we pulled it into the boat along with several more Springers, one of the guys spoke up. "What's the deal with this net?"

"Why don't you tell us?" I responded. "What is the deal with this net? As if you guys don't know?"

"No man, we don't know nothin' about this net." The bigger guy pleaded.

"What's your name? I like talking to people I know."

"Andy, Andy Melankov." He replied.

"So Andy, are you guys competing for set net sites out here now?" I asked, a bit sarcastically. "I mean we run into one net, sit on it and catch you guys running a second one. Kind of unusual isn't it? Then again maybe it's not. No telling how many nets are out on a night when the river is full of fish."

Andy just sat there and stared off into the darkness. Brett and I examined the second net, green cork line, black corks, old style crimped lead line and coincidentally the matching engine head used to anchor the net to the bottom.

"So you guys still in school or what?" Brett asked as he started writing the $2500 citations for Fishing Closed Season.

"My brother is, I'm working at the mill. Got to be there at 7:00 AM or the boss will be pissed." Andy replied.

"Fortunately for you guys, you are local. Otherwise you would be going to the slammer to post bail."

We left them off near their home and issued the citations and receipt for the fish and the nets. Then it was off to return downriver to the boathouse at Astoria, clean the boat, put the nets away at the highway shop and enter the information into evidence. By the time we finished it was daylight, time to head out to sell the fish to a wholesale fish dealer. The money from the sales of illegal fish went to the State General Fund. The two were later convicted in District Court. Time and memory has erased the result of the verdict.

Sports fishing violations

Not to be outdone by the illegal netters. Illegal sport gear fishermen (I won't call them sportsmen) were always there to hold up their end of the pipe. If there was a way to angle illegally that had not been thought of I don't know what it could be. On a hot summer day below The Dalles Dam, I stopped by to look at the fish ladders and the giant spillway that was always gushing water into the river below. Just the sight of it was cooling as I sat there and tried to imagine what it had been like before the thundering Celilo Falls and the Long Narrows Rapid had been stilled by the concrete Hydro Power Dam that now formed the pool of calm water all the way up to Preachers Eddy just below John Day Dam.

The area I was looking at is closed to all fishing, angling and entry by boat. I was surprised to see a small splash as if someone had tossed a rock into the water from just below the ladder entrance. There were Willow bushes clustered near the mouth of Fifteenmile Creek and as I put my binoculars on the bushes I spotted a head of a person just barely hidden by the thick leaves. As I concentrated on the spot I saw a fishing rod sticking up and a line entering the river near where I had seen the splash. It wasn't long before the rod bent over heavily and the figure could be seen reeling and pulling on the rod with a heavy fish on the end of his line. He was oblivious to anything above him and I got out of my truck and walked down the gravel path to the river bank. Just as

I got there he landed a nice 4-5 foot sturgeon, unhooked it and tossed it behind him in the weeds. I figured that was enough so I made my presence known and introduced myself. "State Police, do you mind telling me what you are doing here?"

He nearly fell over with surprise and quickly realized he was caught with nowhere to go but through me. "Officer, I didn't know you were here!" he stated.

"I kind of figured that." I replied. "So how has the fishing been today?"

He gave me that "gee I'm screwed!" look and kind of shrugged as he tossed his head toward the brush behind him. A quick look determined he had three large Sturgeon lying in the grass already dried from the noonday sun.

"Well the way I see it, we have Angling Closed Area and Waste of Game Fish, because these fish are not going to make it." I said.

"No, no Officer, I can get them back in the water and revive them!" he almost begged.

"You're wasting you time and mine, but go ahead and try while I write the Citations." I answered.

The last fish caught took little coaching and immediately swam off back into the cool depths. The next fish was dry and barely motionless as he waded in knee deep and began stroking the sides with water to build up the slime. Surprisingly the fish began finning then undulating and with a splash dove off to join the other. The same thing happened with the third fish as it also swam off after some finessing by the fisherman.

I was amazed by the resilience of the fish and the ability of the fisherman to get the fish back into the water relatively unscathed and left him with only one citation and sent him on his way.

We would periodically check sport fishermen we suspected of taking oversize Sturgeon from the pools behind the dams. These were old fish, some probably over 70 years of age that had survived since before the dams were built and had also ingested every chemical substance that had been released into the river including radioactive chemicals from Hanford Nuclear Reservation far upstream. NMFS was doing tissue studies on the resident Sturgeon populations and told us some real horror stories of the residual effects of chemical pollution on these prehistoric fish. We dropped hints to the fishermen that we could see them at night because they "glowed in the dark" from eating these large illegal fish. Any tactic to discourage poachers was fair as far as we were concerned.

My wife worked at The Dalles High School for the Athletic Director, Art Bull. Art and I became great friends and shared the love of the outdoors and fishing. One day I was sitting at my desk that looked out at the foot of The Dalles Dam about 300 yards away. Below The Dalles Dam was a very deep hole surrounded by rocks on three sides. It held huge Sturgeon and was a popular angling spot for local fishermen. I saw three people fishing off the rocks and decided to put the binoculars on them to get a better look. One of the men had a large fish hooked and was struggling to get it under control. I then realized it was Art who had the fish on. My binoculars had grids on the lens that went vertical as well as horizontal. Art finally had the fish under control and got it into shallow water. The men held the fish in shallow water as they measured it. I took mental note of the number of grid lines the fish fit into. Knowing Art was 6"2" tall, he fit almost exactly the same number of grid lines vertically that the Sturgeon fit horizontally. The men released the huge fish back into the depths and I went back to whatever I was doing.

Several days later I ran into Art and asked him if he had been fishing.

"Yep and you should have seen the Sturgeon I landed!" he exclaimed.

"I did and it was 6'2" long." I replied, taking my best guess.

"How did you know that? Art asked. "I never saw you anywhere around."

I described the day, what he was wearing, who he was with and everything about the fish. He didn't know whether to believe me or not until I explained the situation. The guess about the length was just plain luck but Art still enjoys telling the story to anyone who will listen.

The hooker and the Sturgeon

I imagine you are thinking this is just another story about a fisherman and a Sturgeon. Well as it happened, we were using covert operators in the Portland area to determine if buyers would purchase illegal fish. We had an old but nice Chevy pickup that looked nothing like a police rig and brought in an Officer from out of town to see what he could find out. One of our river patrols had found a freshly killed oversize Sturgeon that had somehow cracked its boney head and beached itself. Other than being dead it was in pretty good shape. We decided to use it and see if anyone in the fish business would buy it. The Officer took it to several known dealers and either got turned down or run off. In one case the owner called our office to report the fish and our undercover man. We felt pretty good about the fact that it was not as easy to sell illegal fish as it had been in the past.

The Officer had a couple more places to visit in North Portland and was traveling along a busy main street in heavy rain. He stopped at a red light and noticed a nice looking young lady standing in the downpour. She waved at him and came over to his vehicle. Not used to the downtown area the Officer simply thought he was being courteous when the young lady asked him if she could get a ride to the next street. She hopped in, shut the door and immediately began asking for money. Now the Officer realized he had made a serious mistake in judgment but did not want to break his cover. He told her she was not going to get any money from him and to get out of the truck.

To his dismay the lady pulled a switchblade and threatened to cut his new seat covers if he didn't giver her $20. She told him her "old man" was watching and would beat her if she came out with no money.

The Officer now was in a predicament he wanted no part of. His focus was on the undercover assignment, not on hooker patrol. He tossed the $20 at her and told her in no uncertain terms to get out. She mumbled something about "crazy rednecks" and walked off.

He came back to the office and told us the story, somewhat perplexed by the incident. He readily admitted he was seriously thinking about the .357 in his shoulder holster but decided there was better way out. We told him to put the $20 on his expense account. We all had a good chuckle and thought about what could have happened. No fish was worth a life.

Just legal 6 foot Sturgeon taken below The Dalles Dam, 1980s. These magnificent huge fish exist in smaller numbers today. Decline is likely to cause the shutdown of both commercial and sport take in the near future.

The Red Handkerchief case

During the majority for my time with the Wildlife division I was stationed on the Columbia River. A good portion of that time was spent in the Astoria area and offshore. I became friends with another Wildlife Officer, Mike Schaecher, who began his career in the 1970s and hailed from my hometown. Mike was younger than me and while growing up, I was acquainted with his family, though I didn't know Mike personally. Through assignments later on I got to know Mike well and found him to be a highly professional and extremely personable Trooper. Mike was so well thought of by his peers at Astoria that they commonly called him Sergeant and sought his advice on many problems.

Mike was also a capable boat operator and usually headed up the offshore fisheries enforcement. He described his early years much the same way I did;

"I was a frustrated Patrol Officer wanting to be a part of the Fish and Wildlife Division in the worst way. Back in the 70s you had to wait for a position either through transfer, retirement, death or know someone in high places to get a game job." In the meantime he did his patrol duties with intermittent jaunts off the beaten path.

His adventures off the highway are best described in his own words.

"It was early in the spring and I was working swing shift on Highway 30 in Clatsop County. The highway parallels the Columbia River where Spring Chinook were on their way upstream from the ocean heading farther than I could dream.

It was a dark and overcast night, not much traffic on the highway so I meandered down to Aldrich Point, a remote boat ramp and old settlement along the seldom used railroad tracks. I wanted, in the worst way, to show I could be a Wildlife Officer or "Game Man" as they were referred to. At Aldrich Point I sat in my patrol car, looking at the river from the boat ramp, listening, wondering if someone might be out there in the dark, drifting with a net, setting an illegal net, poaching. My thoughts were interrupted by headlights coming down the road to the point from the only way in other than the almost impossible dike road. It was a pickup pulling a boat. This was not a sport fisherman. The season was closed. Nor was it a duck hunter. The season was not open. Could this be a poacher?

The driver stopped to talk and turned out to be a local who lived a few miles away. "Sure is dark out here tonight, real quiet on the river." He said.

He didn't know me but I knew him. I mentioned to him that my shift was about over and I needed to head back to the office. I bid him good night and left. Back at the office, I contacted one of the Wildlife Officers and told him what I had seen. The next day the Officer told me he had responded but there was nothing at Aldrich Point when he checked it out. I told him I would continue periodically checking it on my swing shift.

A couple of nights later, on my way back to the office before ending my shift I took a quick trip into Aldrich Point once again. There at the boat ramp was a Ford sedan with California plates. The registered owner had the same last name as the local I had talked to a few nights earlier; the one towing the boat.

When I returned to the office I contacted the Wildlife Officer again about the activity at Aldrich Point. He said he would respond and since my shift was ended I asked if I could ride along. My radar was running! Four eyes, four ears, two thoughts, let's go!

Wanting to be somewhat discrete we got permission from the Game Sergeant to use his unmarked sedan. We were off to

Aldrich Point! When we arrived, the California licensed sedan was still parked at the ramp. Just upriver from the ramp and parallel to the river was an old dirt road. It would be a good place to sit, listen and observe. From there we could contemplate what the suspect(s) might do and what we would do when they returned to the ramp. We parked the car as far back in the overgrown brush as possible and waited.

While we waited we used the opportunity to make a plan based on a variety of scenarios that came to mind. We had no idea if any of the plans we discussed would be used that night. Everything depended on the actions of the suspects. As usual the unexpected happened and we were forced to improvise.

Several hours later we heard the distinct sound of a small boat powered by an outboard motor approaching from upstream toward Aldrich Point. As it neared it slowed and came into shore within fifty feet of where we were parked. We could hear voices but could not understand what they were saying. We heard sounds like bundles of wet paper being dropped on the river bank, three to be exact. So much for planning! The boat then motored slowly down to the boat ramp. One of the suspects got out of the boat, went to the parked sedan, got in and backed down to the ramp. They loaded something in the trunk and then the car pulled slowly away from the ramp. The motorboat left the ramp heading back upstream. The sedan passed the spot where we were hiding. We waited for the boat to move out of hearing distance then started in pursuit of the car. We overtook the car in short order, which was moving at about twenty five miles per hour. I can only imagine what was going through their heads as we came up behind them. There was only one road out and we were behind them! We flipped down the red light mounted just above the windshield and turned on the switch. Nothing happened, no light, no flight just another car following a suspected salmon poacher. Stuff like that happens! My red handkerchief! I pulled it out of my pocket, covered the lens of my 5 cell flashlight and using the button on the switch I mimicked a red flashing light. For the rest of my life I would never experience the reaction a red handkerchief had as it did that night!

It was as if the green flag was waved at the start of Daytona 500 and the race was on! They now knew who we were and we knew they were the ones we wanted. The pursuit took us through the back roads of the diked farmlands of Brownsmead as we headed toward Highway 30. They knew where they were headed and so did we.

They arrived at their residence hardly slowing down, crossing the driveway in a broadside slide around to the back side of the house. As we came to a sliding stop, I bailed out, ran around to the back of the house to see the passenger already running from the car to the far side of the house. I met the driver as he was getting out at the front of the house. When my partner, the Wildlife Officer arrived he told me it was OK to let the suspect up off the ground. I had identified the passenger with my flashlight as a local I had met before. He lived there at the house. We had a conversation with him that night through his bedroom window where he appeared in his union suit. His only comment was "what's going on out there?" as if to insinuate he was never involved, but refused to come out and talk.

The trunk of the car held a dripping wet gillnet, but no fish. The Wildlife Officer and I looked knowingly at each other and with the information we had bid the suspects goodnight.

We returned to Aldrich Point and shortly, near the spot the boat had come close to the bank, we found three burlap sacks containing gillnet caught Spring Chinook.

After daylight the Wildlife Officer, continued the investigation with the assistance of the U.S. Coast Guard, locating another illegally set gillnet just upstream of Aldrich Point. The net was removed and contained a number of dead Salmon that had become entangled in the web.

As a result of the investigation the two suspects contacted were indicted for Felony Fishing Closed Season. The third person operating the boat was not identified but we suspected him to be a well known poacher from Skamokowa, Washington, just across the river. He even showed up at the trial and told me that I spoke the truth. This case was the first Felony fishing case that was prosecuted in Oregon.

As for the red handkerchief, the District Attorney never let me forget it!"

Senior Trooper Mike Schaecher

CHAPTER V

Do you really want to ride along on a Wildlife patrol?

Over the years we were asked to take people along on patrols, mainly media folks so they could experience personally what the Wildlife Officer profession was all about.

One guest, Gale Achterman, the Natural resources Director for the Governor in the early 90s, accompanied us on a boat patrol at the popular and sometimes chaotic Buoy 10 fishery. We suited her up in a full Mustang suit and gave her instructions to hang on as the seas could be rough.

I was accompanied by Sr.Tpr. Rick Pert on the big rigid hull inflatable that was capable of high speeds and heavy seas. We left the marina behind and headed out to the center of the action. Hundreds of sport fishing boats crowded the small area near the deadline making it an impossible task to check them all. We concentrated on boats that appeared to be ill equipped as safety compliance was a big part of our job. After checking several boats and finding insufficient life jackets, no safety equipment, no angling licenses, too many lines, untagged fish, we would cite them and send them back to the marinas to get into compliance.

During one lull in the action Gale asked me why we singled out boats that were, in her words, "In the less affluent class on the water that day?"

I answered that we were there with a minimum amount of manpower and time and it made sense to maximize the effect. To drive home the point we checked a number of the better appointed boats and found few violations if any.

"Experience had shown us that accidents happened more frequently to skippers and boats that did not have proper equipment or maintenance." I explained. "Our job required that we profile much like the Patrol Officers look for reasons to stop suspicious cars on the highways."

She nodded her acquiescence and turned her attention to the unfolding events of the day.

My wife had never ridden on a patrol with me in all the years and I never really thought much about it until I returned for some contract work during hunting season in the Northwest part of the State. She had always been busy raising our three kids or working full time after they were out of school and on their own. I asked her if she would like to go along one night and she readily agreed. I was not expecting anything out of the normal as things were usually pretty quiet. Archery season was in progress and I headed up into the Saddle Mountain unit near the Jewell Wildlife Refuge. It was extremely foggy and wet as well as humid. I covered the gravel roads I was familiar with and as usual nothing was moving. I came off one mainline road just north of the refuge and turned onto Hwy 202. It's a small two lane blacktop from Jewell to Astoria. A number of mainline logging roads spill onto the road and as I drove by one of them I noticed a car parked alongside in the gravel. At 2:00AM it aroused my curiosity and my wife even commented about the car. I continued down the road to the next turnout and pulled off to observe and listen for a while. I had just pulled into the gravel when I noticed a figure coming out of the brush. He was shirtless, disheveled, wild eyed and holding a hunting bow with an arrow knocked in position to shoot. As a former bow hunter, I was well aware of the capability of the bow and arrow especially the razor sharp hunting tips. I jumped out, unsnapped my holstered 357 Magnum and ordered him to put the weapon down. He looked confused and frightened and for a second or two I thought things were going to go bad.

He yelled. "I'm lost. I've been walking around in the woods for hours. I saw some elk back there a ways but it was too dark to shoot!" He sounded confused even about what time it was.

"Man it's two in the morning. It's been too dark to shoot for 8 hours." I answered back. "Now put the bow away and let's get you calmed down."

He complied and just about then several rigs pulled up, one of them belonging to the refuge manager. They had been looking for him also. He was one of their hunting party and they were more than a little concerned for his safety.

After a little conversation, I got back in my truck and they left. I looked at Evelyn and she had this mused look on her face. "Does that happen all the time?" she asked.

"No." I laughed, "Fortunately not. This was just another minor incident." I was glad she got to experience an unusual situation just to validate some of the tales I had brought home over the years.

On another night early in my career, my good friend Dwayne was riding along on patrol near the small town of Timber in the coast range. We were checking out some dead end roads in the summer and things were dry and warm even at midnight. We pulled into a narrow two lane road and found it blocked by a pickup truck. I hit the high beams and rudely interrupted a young couple having a "talk" in the front seat. At least I thought they were talking. He was startled by my high beams and presence, hit the starter and attempted to pull forward. The road was blocked by down trees and he apparently ripped a hole in his gas tank on a stick because suddenly there were flames from under the rig. I yelled at them to get out and looked for my only fire extinguisher. They were both out of the truck and retreated back to my truck as I emptied the contents of the extinguisher on the flames. It was useless and the flames soon spread to the brush nearby. It was time to get out of there and call the fire department. I called it in as we got the two people and ourselves out of the brush patch that was now in flames. Shortly we heard the sirens of the local Fire Department coming to the rescue. They pulled up short and two of the volunteers grabbed a hose and started running toward the blaze. Just like in the movies the hose was not long enough to reach as they came to a sudden and not so graceful stop.

After hooking a second hose to the tanker and reconnecting the two they were able to get to the fire and prevent any further conflagration. The truck was a black burned out shell now as the owner looked it over and tried to estimate his losses.

Dwayne and I were standing to one side as two of the volunteer firemen surveyed the scene and the one with just a few teeth confidently announced, "This looks like a case of arson!"

Dwayne looked at me and just shook his head. I gave my information to the fire chief and we went on our way.

Days off during hunting seasons

Yes there were days off during the long hunting seasons in the 1970s. These were the times we hooked up with our hunting buddies, shared information we had gathered while working and scrambled through the thick brush of the Coast Range to harvest our Deer or Elk before we had to return to patrol. Usually two days was it.

One particular year I had watched a large Bull Elk that had frequented a small clearing visible from only one spot on Hwy 26 near Wolf Creek. Every morning he was there and nothing had disturbed him. Opening morning of Elk season he was gone but having checked the area heavily I knew he had not been harvested and in fact no one had invaded his territory, leaving him to our group. On Monday after opening weekend I took my two day weekend off. I rounded up my Dad and Brother Tom for the hunt and explained to them exactly what I wanted to do and how we would do it. Dad was 69 and not in the best health but he could walk and shoot. I put him on Wolf Creek road, an impassable road to motor vehicles and told him to ease along the road while Tom and I went up the hill to where I had last seen the big Bull.

It was a nice day and we got started just about daylight. Tom stayed on my left and circled lower on the far side of the hill while I went straight to the top. 50 yards from the top I heard an animal break out and head down my side of the hill toward Dad. I whistled to Tom and saw him motioning he too had heard the animal go. We both headed down the hill toward the road fully expecting to head off Dad and maybe get a shot at the Bull before he crossed the road into Wolf Creek bottom lands between us and Hwy 26.

When we got to the road there was no sign of the old man other than foot prints in the mud heading up the road. We ran to the next curve and then saw him peering into the brush on the downhill side with his trusty old octagon barrel 30-30 Winchester at ready. I whistled softly and he looked back then pointed into the brush signaling Bull with his outstretched fingers over his head. I wondered why he hadn't shot and as we approached he put his finger to his lips to signal silence. I was ready with my 338 Mag for any sign of the Bull. I whispered to him asking where the bull was and he answered that it was close by having crossed 50 yards in front of him. I asked why he didn't shoot. He explained the bull had his head down and he could not get the shot he wanted. Dad had always preferred a head shot.

Tom and I bailed off the road into the brush in the direction Dad said the Bull went. I knew he would be moving and we had to catch up if we wanted a shot. 50 yards into the brush it got very wet and spongy and fresh tracks were everywhere. Suddenly the brush exploded as elk went all directions, none with antlers, but I knew the bull would be close by. We kept on the trail and cautiously moved forward. Probably 5 minutes later two quick shots shattered the stillness and my heart sank. I knew what lay ahead. We came to a clearing and there was the Bull, on his side, dead as a post and a young hunter standing over as if guarding it. I congratulated him on his kill. He told us his Dad had brought him up Hwy 26 and dropped him off just past the Junction of Timber Road where we had gone in. He picked a stump and sat down waiting no more than 20 minutes before the big Bull walked right into him. All we could do was congratulate him and wish him luck getting it back to the highway. I was disgusted and discouraged that all the planning had resulted in a lucky hunter being in the right place at the right time.

That same year we managed to fill one tag in our other party, but elk hunting is that way, especially when you have limits on your time. My partner, Bob, managed to draw blood on a spike later that year but two days of tracking produced nothing as the blood trail got thinner and thinner.

We met some interesting characters that year; Half Track, The Mountain Man, and others whose names escape me.

One group of Air Traffic Controllers hunted and camped near old Camp Olsen at the summit of Hwy 26. We were always welcome at their very comfortable camp that boasted a fireplace, iron cook stove, bunk beds, felt floors and liquor supply. They invited us for Thanksgiving dinner that included Honey glazed ham, roast turkey with all the trimmings and assortment of pies. It was a great place to stop and take a break from the 12 hour days. No one camps like that anymore as most of the private land has been locked up and camping is prohibited. I really feel that the large number of camps high in the mountains prevented much of the spotlighting and night hunting activity that goes on now.

It was not the least unusual to check 8-12 bull elk opening weekend from the old Rock Creek Railroad mainline that extended from Sunset Highway to Keasey. Dozens of camps dotted the old clearings left from when the logging camps moved out years before. Many of the old trestles still remained intact from the logging railroads that criss crossed the mountains. The brave would drive the trestles careful to stay on the planks lest they plunge off 50 or more feet to the bottom. I tried it successfully once and never again pushed my luck.

Several years of Elk hunting resulted in a couple of antlerless Elk taken but no big Bulls.

This year I have been successful in drawing a second season elk permit from that Saddle Mountain area, a three point or better unit. I have only been successful in taking a branch antlered bull Elk one time in my life. I am anticipating one more chance before I hang up the rifle for good.

I am looking forward to hunting the areas I used to work so many years ago. They have changed dramatically, with plantations of Douglas fir grown to harvest size, logged and replanted since I first worked there 40 years ago.

❖

CHAPTER VI

Shellfish Harvesting and the "other" side of Law Enforcement

Nothing brings out the greed or voracity in people like harvesting shellfish. It doesn't seem to matter where the limit is placed. People will exceed. Wildlife Officers are often faced with the choice of calling it a mistake or simply a willful violation of the rules.

One day I was working at Netarts Bay just out of Tillamook. The low tide had drawn hundreds of clam diggers to the area and most were leaving the area with legal limits. I checked one man and he pointed out two men far out in the middle of the bay that he claimed had badly exceeded the limit of 18 clams per person.

"They know you are here and they aren't coming in till you leave." He advised me. "I'm a little concerned because the tide is already moving in!"

I moved my truck down the road behind some trees and walked back to the spot where I could see the two with my binoculars. They were now walking toward me, still several hundred yards away, carrying obviously heavy buckets. They had two channels to cross before they hit dry sand and the tide was beginning to come in fast. The first channel was waist deep and both of them made it across with some difficulty. Now I was becoming concerned because the next channel was deeper. I considered calling the Coast Guard when the first man crossed with the water up to his shoulders. The second man entered the water and immediately lost his balance and his hold on the bucket of clams. He began swimming and finally reached the shallow water. His partner went back in, retrieved the lost bucket, clams still intact, and they continued on toward the shore.

I waited, relieved they were both out of danger, till they reached the road and walked up to confront them. They were soaking wet, but it was a warm summer day and they showed no ill effects from the dunking. I asked to see their licenses and commented on their little foray in the deep water, pointing out that by now the water was rushing in and far deeper than it had been when they crossed. They just shrugged it off and did their best to convince me they were in no danger.

"You two were the last ones off the tide flats. You must have had trouble filling your limits." I commented.

At the same time I began counting their obvious over limits of bay clams. When I finished counting, one was over his limit by 32 clams and the other by 35! I didn't have to inform them of their mistake. They knew what they had done.

"What are you going to do to us now?" One of them asked in broken English.

"Well both of you are getting citations for Exceeding the bag limit. And the excess clams will be seized and donated to the jail to feed prisoners." I advised.

The older of the two, who had gone swimming and lost his clams could not understand English and was being told by his companion what the consequences would be. He immediately started arguing, swearing and kept shouting, "No ticket, no ticket!"

His companion tried unsuccessfully to calm him down. I had already secured their licenses and was writing the citations. When I explained the procedure he threw the ticket back at me again exclaiming, "No ticket!"

I placed the citation in the car and told his companion to explain to his friend that they must follow the instructions on the citations. When I left, the older man was still shouting what I assume were obscenities in my direction. I guess he just wanted more than his legal share of clams.

An old friend of mine, who has passed away, used to tell me how he would never keep broken clams. The law required sport harvesters to keep any and all Razor clams they dug. I advised him that he was going to get caught if he didn't change his ways.

One day after a clamming excursion he related his story to me regarding a close call with the law. He was Razor clamming by himself pretty close to the surf line. He was into a good number of clams and in his haste broke a nice one in two. Just as he was about to put it back in the hole and bury it he glanced up and saw brown booted feet several yards away. He looked up straight into the eyes of a rather large Wildlife Officer. "Dang I hate it when that happens." He exclaimed to the Officer tossing the battered clam into his container.

The Officer smiled and replied, "Good call!"

Toward the end of my career, I was delegated to troubleshooting duties out of District Headquarters. "Rogue" Wildlife Officers became my responsibility. Not that any of them seriously crossed the lines of written policies but some of them just needed a gentle reminder of how it should be done. We received a complaint from two Shellfish harvesters that a uniformed Officer had used abusive language and ordered them to come up from the beach to his position rather than going to them.

I made the trip to Astoria, contacted the Officer and invited myself along on patrol. We discussed the incident and how it should have been handled as we approached the tidal flats where clam diggers were busy once again. I went to check on two who were coming off the beach and determined they were legal. I returned to the truck and got in when I observed the Officer heading my way with a commercial digger.

Norm was being as nice as he could be and I could see the muscular digger was being particularly obnoxious. He log book was not up to date, grounds for a violation notice or at the very least a warning.

Norm marched him to my open window and explained the problem. The digger was having none of it and continued his tirade of obscene remarks about enforcement in general. I wanted Norm to handle it all the way. The man then proceeded to declare he could whip both of our "asses". At that point I had enough and got out of the truck, towering at least a foot over his 5"5" frame.

"Take off that badge and I'll kick your ass right here and now!" the man retorted.

I started to pull my badge off and all hell was about to break loose when Norm calmly stepped in and parted us. He handled the situation calmly, issued a warning to the commercial digger and sent him on his way.

Then Norm looked at me and wryly grinned." Nice move Sergeant."

"You better keep this under your hat, Norm." I cautioned. "We wouldn't want anyone getting the idea that this is the way to handle situations now, would we?"

When I returned to District Headquarters I reported the situation had been taken care of.

Another incident that stands out in my mind was a clam digging foray to Netarts at Happy Camp. It was one of my Parents favorite places to stay and they invited us down. My three young ones, Greg, Kris and Tom were in their early teens and enjoyed the outings as much as I did. I took them down to the beach and set about finding clams for them to dig. The rules were, they had to dig their own and each had their own container. Greg and Tom caught on quickly but Kris decided it was too much "yuck factor" so reluctantly pulled just a few clams.

My Dad, and Brother in Law, Ernie, were in the water digging bay clams so I joined them. We came up with more than a few empty shells and tossed them over our shoulders. A few of the clams also came up broken but still had to be kept, no exceptions.

When I came back to the kids I inspected their catch, counted the clams and washed them off. We were still short of limits but they were done.

We climbed the hill back to the cars and motel. My Mom was sitting on a bench watching and motioned to me that a State Trooper was waiting in the parking lot wanting to talk to me about something.

I thought maybe it was one of my acquaintances so I walked over to see what he wanted. The conversation went something like this.

"I've been watching you digging clams and I'm not very pleased with what I saw." He said.

"And just what did you see?" I asked.

"You know what you were doing sir, I don't think I have to explain it to you." He shot back.

I was rather irritated by the way he had come on to me and was struggling to hang on to my temper. "Maybe you better explain it, because I don't know what you're talking about."

He then shifted the conversation, "I understand you are a State Police Sergeant. How do you think this would go over with my Sergeant? I don't think you set a very good example here."

By this time I'd had enough of the dancing around and innuendos and replied, "Either write me a citation for what you think you saw or leave me alone! I've just about had enough!"

The Trooper slammed his citation book on the hood of his patrol car, got in and spun gravel out of the parking lot and back onto the road. My family, observing from a distance, was puzzled at what had happened and so was I. I tried piecing together what happened and what made this Trooper draw the conclusion that he had.

What I think happened was; the Trooper saw us digging in the surf, tossing empty shells back, which he assumed were broken clams, then saw us counting the kids clams again assuming we were dividing up clams so everyone had a limit. Remember, everyone did not have a limit?

Again the word ASSUME came into play. In the Police Academy, years ago the old Captain admonished us to never ASSUME! Because you make an ASS out of U and ME!

I called the District Wildlife Lieutenant and explained the situation to him including the fact I did not enjoy having my short vacation ruined. He advised me he would look into it.

Later I got a call from the Supervisor of the young Trooper. He explained that a lack of experience and an eagerness to uphold the rules accounted for the young man's actions. I explained to my family that State Troopers don't normally respond like that. My concern was the fact that if he acted in that manner to another member of his own Department, how would he act toward a member of the recreating public? Courtesy and tact went a long way in law enforcement. It was always a matter of protocol to introduce oneself to the violator and politely explain why they were being stopped or investigated.

It was important to me to stress wildlife law adherence to my children and my friend's children as they were growing up. As several stories in Outlaws in the Big Woods pointed out, when you wanted the truth, ask the kid.

My oldest son Greg worked to get his hunters safety certificate and after a couple of unsuccessful years hunting he drew a tag for "one deer" in the Dufur Mill area of the Mt. Hood National Forest outside The Dalles. We hunted some old abandoned logging roads in the area. I was not carrying a gun and wanted him to have the only shot. A large branch antlered Buck suddenly stepped out in front of us about 40 yards away. I silently pointed at the deer and gave him the shoot sign. He looked back at me as if to question. I then raised my voice and said "shoot'.

The deer jumped and bounded away without a shot being fired. I asked him why he didn't shoot.

"It was a buck." He replied.

"I know it was." I said.

"I thought the tag was for a doe only." He said.

Frustrated as I was, I realized he had hesitated because he was not sure of his target, one of the first rules in hunting. He was young and inexperienced but did not succumb to "buck fever". And it was only a deer! There would be more opportunities. I was proud of the kid! My mistake was not briefing him fully on what the limits of the tag were.

My kids shared many good days of fishing and hunting while they were growing up. My younger son Tom never let me forget his first Steelhead.

We were Shad fishing below the John Day Dam and they were having a great time reeling in one after the other of the fighting little fish. Suddenly Tom's rod bent over and the line screamed off his reel. I knew it was no Shad, so went over to help him. He was probably 10 at the time and had been out Salmon fishing in the ocean numerous times on our boat. He did a good job reeling in the fish and as I netted it I recognized it as a Steelhead. I thought the season was closed, so sadly I had to release the fish. Senior Trooper Fred Patton was working the area later that day and I told him the story of Tom's fish.

He looked at me in his quizzical way and said, "Steelhead just opened today."

Tom's reply was, "Dad, you released my first Steelhead ever!"

I replied, "I'm sorry Tom." It was always better to err on the right side of the law.

Fred got a good laugh out of that and another story to tell about his Sergeant.

My Dad was not a big fan of fishing until he retired. He then took to it with a passion, all sorts of fishing, crabbing, clamming, any excuse to use his little 15 foot Starcraft.

He called once and invited us to join him and my Mother and another family friend at Tillamook. They were harvesting soft-shell clams in the upper bay at Memaloose. Now his method was to take a couple passengers out to the mud flats and return to the ramp and pick up two more. Clams were plentiful and the limit was 36. At low tide the flats were barely navigable but the old 18 horse had shear pins and a supply of 10 penny nails and heavy pliers kept the prop turning. Shear a pin and tilt the motor, shove in a new "nail", bend it over and continue on.

I volunteered to go get the next load of diggers, my two sons, Greg, Tom, daughter Kris and my wife, Evelyn. We only had to replace two shear pins before we got to the flats. Time was running out and in an hour the tide would be returning so we dug our limits and took the bags and kids back to the ramp. My Mom and friend stayed to finish up and Dad went back to get them. I watched as he broke two more pins on the flats as the tide began to turn. I could barely see them from the ramp and without a boat there was little I could do but wait.

Finally I saw them returning to the ramp walked down to meet them. Mom was mad as heck at Dad and the friend was laughing and shaking his head. The tide had started back over the flats, and was knee deep by the time he got the boat to them. Mom was adamant that was the last time she would be clam digging with my Dad. She insisted they could have drowned or worse! Dad just brushed it off claiming the boat would have floated right to her. She brought it up to him more than once in later years.

Dad was a little over confident with his boat and although he always wore life jackets, at times he failed to pay attention to the weather. I was working at the coast one day and I knew he would be crabbing in Tillamook Bay so I drove on up to Garibaldi. I drove to the end of the pier and was watching the heavy winds build up whitecaps on the bay. I didn't expect to see any boats on the water but sure enough, there was one little red Starcraft bobbing up and own as they retrieved their crab pots! Waving and honking I was finally able to attract his attention and direct him to shore. As usual Dad was nonchalantly explaining how they had been out crabbing when it got rough and they were just picking up the gear. I calmly explained to him, that the crab pots were not worth his or someone else's life. A few years later at 85 he decided it was time to give up the sport he loved. My two Brothers and I accompanied him on one last trip crabbing at Nehalem just shortly before he died in his sleep.

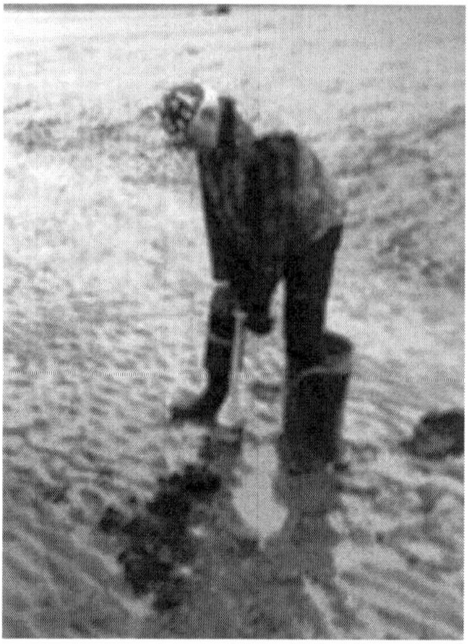

CHAPTER VII
More cases from the woods
The three fingered Logger

Early in my career in Wildlife Enforcement I was relaxing at home by the fire, when I received a call from Senior Trooper Dan Primus from the Astoria area. He was chasing leads on an illegal cow Elk case that had occurred in the Elsie area off Hwy 26. Information had led him to the residential area where I lived and he needed help to find his way around the many streets in Aloha, Oregon.

I told him to come by and pick me up, always anxious to get in on some big game action. He had the name and address of one person from a license number on a car that had been seen near the area of the kill. It was all he had but there was other information about the description of the shooters. Knock and talk was the method of operation in those days. Today it is discouraged and quite frankly against policy to walk up to someone's home knock on the door and have a chat. But armed with information unknown to the suspect it often resulted in confessions coming forth and implications of others involved.

We located the home of the registered owner of the suspect vehicle and a quick glance at the truck as we went by with our flashlight showed some blood stains in the bed. Now this fact alone during hunting season was hardly evidence of illegal activity. Some of these guys were hard core hunters, going out to help their buddies recover animals and retrieving their own.

We knocked on the door, introduced ourselves and were invited in to ask a "few questions".

The suspect, "Bill" we will call him for the sake of the story, was at first non committal about having taken any animals. We asked about the blood in his truck bed and he mumbled something about how it may have been from deer season that closed a week earlier. Dan told him his rig had been seen in the Elsie area during the first season Elk hunt and asked if he had a first season tag. He replied that he did not have a tag but was helping a friend hunt.

Small talk ensued about their hunt when Dan suddenly said, "Hey how about calling your friend, John and can go over and talk to him also?"

Bill was caught off guard and replied to the effect that "John" was not with him, it was his other friend Dave. Dan looked at me and winked.

"Oh I thought you said John was with you, I must have misunderstood." Dan swiftly replied. Now he had the first name of Bill's companion and had not had to ask for it. I was enjoying the way Dan was leading him around the story. Bill agreed to call Dave at home for Dan and when Dave answered Bill told him there was a cop that wanted to talk to him.

Dan took the phone and began talking to Dave explaining how we had been talking to Bill about the hunting trip and we would like to come over to his house right away and look at the Elk he had. I had to hide my surprise and watched as Bill's eyes grew wider. I could read his thoughts. "How the hell did he know?"

Dan told Bill to lead us over to Dave's house acting as if he knew where to go in any case. Dan was filling me in on what I had already observed. It had worked better than either of us could have imagined. We arrived at Dave's house and he was waiting with the garage door open.

We again introduced ourselves to Dave and he meekly led us into the garage where several quarters of Elk were hanging. "My wife is already pissed about this, I guess I should have known better."

"Okay guys, now let's start from the beginning and get all the facts out. I know a bit about what happened as you already know so don't be trying to snowball us." Dan advised.

I suspected Dan still had a little more up his sleeve. And he did.

"You two didn't do all this by yourselves now did you?" Dan asked. "I want to know about the other guy who left the scene. All I know is he had two fingers missing on one hand and was dressed in logging attire. Help me out here and it can go better for both of you."

These two were far from the usual hard core poachers and saw a way out of this mess. "All I know about that guy was his name is Gordon. He shot the two cows and we came out of the brush nearby. He was by himself and offered us one of the cows if we would help him get them to the logging road and his truck. He assured us there were never any Officers in that area and all we had to do was make it home and nothing more would happen. We talked to him while we were getting the elk field dressed and loaded and he told us he lived in the Seaside area and worked for Crown logging."

"Ok" Dan replied. "I need a description of his rig and a little more about his features and if we catch up with him, I'll make a note to the Judge how you co operated with us. In the meantime we will issue both of you citations for Unlawful Possession of Cow Elk Closed Season. Notice you are not being charged with killing the elk, just possession."

Dan and I both knew the penalties were the same but it sounded better and made them feel a little better. We seized the meat and left the two somewhat dazed and confused hunters, wishing they had never seen the logger.

Armed with the meat, the descriptions and information the two had given us, Dan called me several days later and happily announced he had located the three fingered logger and when confronted with the evidence and statements from the two accomplices readily confessed to killing the two cow elk. It was a masterful piece of investigative and interrogative work I learned from Dan that night.

Unfortunately as mentioned earlier this technique is no longer sanctioned by the Department. Procedures are spelled out in painstaking detail, maybe because of deviation from the rules of evidence gathering, maybe just things change over the years. It was nevertheless an interesting time to be a Wildlife Officer.

Some of us were discussing the "OLD WAYS" and counting our fortunes for having been there and done that. Not that we were somehow tougher or braver, or worked smarter but certain things had to be handled with what was available to us at the time. We didn't have computers in our vehicles, half of the time the radio was out of frequency range. We made numerous stops in the middle of the night, in the woods, on back secluded roads, with no backup. We never wore bulletproof vests, they weren't even available and once they were, there were no requirements to wear something that uncomfortable. While most of the stops were routine, a few of them made the hair stand up on your neck, put you on edge, wondering if you were going to get out of this one with your life.

Still it was the greatest job in the world for most of us. At our yearly inservice training one year at Monmouth Western Oregon College Campus, the staff politely asked us if we could hold our breaks between classes away from the hall where the regular students traveled. They advised us the staff and students were intimidated by all the uniform Troopers. We agreed and one of the young Troopers who worked for me at the time commented about it.

"What's their problem?" he asked.

I glanced at the shoulder patch on our sleeves and replied, "See that patch? It's the insignia of one of the finest, toughest, no nonsense agencies in this State since the 1930 when it was formed. You may not realize what it means yet but to those who grew around the badge and insignia, it commands respect. Yes some are slightly intimidated by it until they need our help. Then it gives us just the edge we need to stay in control of a bad situation."

Mike

While writing about my time spent in The Dalles I neglected to acknowledge one of the most affable and professional Troopers I ever had occasion to work with. Sr. Tpr. Mike Caldwell had transferred to The Dalles late in my tenure to fill a vacancy from Tillamook where I had first met him. The last several years in The Dalles were years I preferred to forget but Mike was one of those Officers who set high standards for himself and drove himself every day to as near perfection as he could attain while still bringing a sense of humor and easiness to a hard working group of Troopers.

He fit right in from the start and as usual with a new assignment came a brand new shiny 4 wheel drive vehicle that he tried his best to keep that way.

Sooner or later, Wildlife Officers had to yield their feelings to the inevitable fact that those new shiny rigs were going to get beaten by rocks, mud, tree branches on narrow roads and sometimes ornery cattle dogs, some of which actually enjoyed trying to chew off hub Caps and license plates if An Officer lingered long enough at a ranch along the way.

An initiation of sorts also was dished out by other Troopers who callously would kick dents into the shiny hubcaps of new pickups and deny it ever happened. What happened to Mike was a little short of cruelty when he showed up at one of our yearly road checks in his new rig, parked it and joined the parade of hunters stopping to be checked near Bear Springs. Mike was hard into checking and not paying attention as several other Troopers swapped out his new hubcaps with some severely beaten ones from one of the old vehicles on the scene. They also filled the back of his pickup bed with dirty gravel, stick and leaves, giving it that "seasoned look' and went on about their business. Mike soon discovered his trashed rig and could not imagine his friends and fellow Troopers doing this. Mike was on the verge of rage when finally his clean new hubcaps were returned to him and brooms deployed to sweep out the load of forest trash.

Every Trooper at The Dalles and Hood River had at one time or another had the unpleasant task of loading and unloading the cumbersome 24 foot Custom Bow picker that served as one of the patrol boats. The easiest way to load the boat was to position the trailer slightly in the water and power the big heavy craft onto the skids. A set of controls were located on the bow of the boat and also in the cabin.

We had taken the boat out on the river and returned to the ramp. Mike was begging me to take over the loading duties as he had never done it before and did not want to try it in front of several people who were watching there at the ramp. I assured him he could load it and now was as good a time as any. He positioned himself at the wheel and began the loading process. Several near misses, backing off, attempting another run only added to his frustration. At the bow controls it was difficult to tell just where the stern of the boat was but Mike persisted. One attempt was working nicely when he suddenly moved the wheel as the boat was settling onto the trailer. The stern came around and set the boat on the trailer –sideways. Now it required backing the trailer in to deeper water to float the boat off the side rails. I could tell Mike was getting frustrated and pissed at the same time, begging me to finish loading the boat. One more pass put the boat neatly between the rails and on the trailer. I congratulated him on the fine job although I don't think he accepted it graciously mumbling something about getting even someday.

The Quack attack

Mike and one other Trooper were working the brushy shoreline above the Dalles Dam near Rabbit Islands and discovered a set net during closed season. After a little more searching they discovered the suspected netter asleep in a sleeping bag near the net. This was late at night and they wanted to catch the suspect in the act of pulling the net as often they simply claimed no knowledge of the nets and the cases went down the drain. They settled back in the brush and waited for dawn.

Dawn came and so did the Sun but the Suspect remained fast asleep. Desperate to figure out a way to wake him and catch him pulling the net, the other Trooper produced a duck call from his pocket. A series of loud calls and quacks pierced the morning silence and finally the suspect stirred in his sleeping bag, realized where he was and the need to get his net retrieved and be on his way. He had just retrieved the net when Mike and Bob stepped out of the brush and apprehended yet another illegal set netter.

Once again innovation paid off.

I left The Dalles after 8 years for another much more desired assignment in Portland but regrettably left behind some friends I had made including Troopers like Mike.

Who loosed the goose?

Several USFWS Officers accompanied us on a case on Sauvie Island. We had reports of excessive over limits on one private club that was surrounded on two sides by public land. 4 of us worked our way in before daylight and hidden by camouflage waited for the shoot to begin. There were 6 shooters in three pit blinds and the geese were flying as dawn broke. Time after time they set their wings and dove into the decoys. Shotguns blasted as geese fell to the ground. As they approached the two goose limit of 12 a large flock came in. We knew that at least three more geese were killed than there were hunters to account for them. We moved out of our positions and rounded up the hunters. At first there was some shuffling from blind to blind until everyone got the word to stop and listen. Dave, one of the Federal Agents explained what we had observed and asked to see all the geese. After the count there were two more geese then allowed but we all agreed there should be one more. The group introduced themselves as Attorneys and insisted they had produced all of the birds. We searched the blinds and surrounding area and were still unconvinced but went ahead and began writing citations for exceeding the bag limit. One Attorney appeared uneasy and was shifting position when the head of a wounded Canada goose stuck his head out from under his coat and HONKED!

Everyone burst out laughing except the red faced Attorney. Several weeks later they appeared in District Court in Portland. We testified to what we had seen and emphasized the deliberate attempt to hide the evidence. The Judge was laughing and commented "Sounds like someone got goosed" as he pronounced the guilty verdict.

Lawyer stories were always kind of satisfying especially when they were on the wrong side of the case. A rather prominent Attorney from The Dalles was relating a story to me one day about a float they had made on the Deschutes River earlier. He was describing the area just above the mouth and how they had spotted a flock of Snow Geese just ahead. He then related how he had gotten out of the boat and made a fine stalk on the Geese. All the time he was talking I was thinking about the constant presence in that area of a group of Swans. I let him finish his story and when he got to the part about harvesting two of them if he had properly identified the Snow Geese.

"Oh yes I know what Snow Geese look like. They don't have black wingtips, do they?" He replied hesitating slightly.

"Do you know or are you guessing?" I asked.

As I explained the difference, his face got rather pale and I could tell he was getting very uncomfortable.

"How did they taste?" I asked.

He stammered and mumbled something unintelligible and assured me he would be more careful in the future. I suggested a bird identification class may be helpful also.

Multnomah County has one of the largest Marine Patrol Divisions in the State. They cover most of the Columbia River and Willamette River around Portland. Once a year they would invite me to come in and refresh their Officers on Wildlife violations they were likely to encounter. They seldom checked angling licenses unless it was in the course of a boat inspection.

One Officer remarked about a problem they had during waterfowl seasons around Sauvie Island. Several large marinas had developed in the area and resident ducks and Canada Geese became domesticated by being fed regularly from the houses on the river. He related one problem that involved a boatload of hunters passing by one of the marinas populated by quite a few Mallards. While they were sensible enough not to shoot around the houses, they tossed bread crumbs out of the boat luring the ducks downriver, and then shot them, infuriating the homeowners.

The Officers were unsure as to the legality and what action they could have taken. I explained to them the baiting laws of the Waterfowl regulations. It was one of the most classic cases of baiting waterfowl I had ever heard. But it pointed out once again the complexities of enforcement of all the laws. They had little training on Wildlife regulations and could not be expected to know every law on the books. The next time would be different!

Lost in the Dark

Leryl, Don and I were checking on information received of a group of hunters who consistently hunted both seasons without proper tags. We staked out an area near Vernonia where the group was reported to be hunting. I donned camouflage gear and carried a bucket to look like a mushroom picker. We had heard several shots in a canyon off Pittsburgh Road and thought there might be some animals down. I was skirting a hillside in a fairly open area when I heard someone call out a name. I answered and waited for more. Hearing none I moved on and then noticed a hunter moving along below me. He had seen me and knew I was not a hunter, and then called out to me asking if I had seen his partner.

"Nope, I'm just hunting mushrooms. What's up?" I asked nonchalantly as I could, not wanting to make him think I was interested.

"Oh I just got a couple of Elk down in the canyon and I need him to bring his tag(s)." He volunteered.

I wanted to get closer so I could identify him if he ran, so I just worked my way slowly to him and then pulled back my coat to show him my badge. I radioed Don who was nearby and asked him to come over.

The hunter was cooperating fully by now and knew he was in trouble. He said he had no tag as he had hunted the East side and just wanted to help out his buddies.

Don arrived on scene and took over the investigation. It was obvious from the beginning the Elk were going to have to be taken care of. It was late in the afternoon so Don volunteered to return to the Elk with the hunter and get them dressed so they would not spoil. The other hunters apparently got word and left the area. Leryl and I remained at the top of the canyon and when darkness fell, Don had still not come out of the canyon. We had radios and finally made contact with him. He advised they were now headed uphill but neither had flashlights with them and it was very dark. We stayed in contact and helped by using our strobe lights and electronic sirens to keep them oriented. Once they were close enough to see the lights, Leryl took a couple of flashlights and headed down into the canyon to help them out. When they all got back to the top, they were describing the total darkness, having to feel their way along through the brush and trees with outstretched hands and the occasional dim light of Dons cell phone.

The hunter and two other members of his party were contacted the next day, assisted in getting the elk to thee top of the canyon and received summons to appear in court for their efforts.

ATV Games

One of the more enjoyable times I had enforcing Wildlife laws was the period of time when I came back from Alaska and worked in the Access and Habitat program. This program had its beginnings when retired Major Walt Hershey suggested we begin meetings on a monthly basis with District Attorneys, Land

Owners, Judges, ODFW, Division of State Lands and anyone else interested in solving problems on private land.

Locking up private lands had become more and more common due to vandalism, theft and generally tearing up fragile ecosystems with hundreds of four wheel drive rigs even though the State had set aside areas for their use.

With an added charge on Game Tags enough money was generated to hire full time/temporary retired Wildlife Officers to patrol these private lands under agreement during the hunting seasons. As a result the gates were opened and more land was accessible to the hunters, enforcement action could be taken without the need for landowner complaints being filed and problems were more easily addressed.

I went to work initially in the Saddle Mountain area, then in the Columbia County area after moving to Columbia City. One of the worst areas for ATV travel violations was less than three miles from my house in the Maple Hill and Canaan Road area. It was not uncommon to encounter ATV groups every day however catching them was another problem altogether. ATVs could easily run off though the timber and disappear in minutes. Four wheel drive pickups had to stay on the road.

Another problem area was the Pisgah Home road above Scappoose. Here the road had been torn up so bad it had become a danger. ATVs worked their Way up from Dutch Canyon through second growth forest and culminated on a steep bank before climbing onto the main road. They had cut a trench with spinning wheels almost halfway across the main road. Unsuspecting drivers could at minimum lose their front end or be tossed over a hundred foot embankment. I concentrated my efforts on those areas and on one rainy Sunday was accompanied by Bill Monroe, Oregonian Outdoor Writer and longtime friend. Longview Fiber Security Officer had the camera crew following. We encountered several rigs with ATVs loaded onto trailers and cautioned them against any use on private lands in the area. Several of them chose to leave.

We had almost reached the junction of the Gunter Mainline logging road and as we rounded a corner we were greeted by perhaps 20 plus ATVs behind a locked gate. Several were in the act of jumping back onto the road we were traveling by running over a dirt berm placed there specifically to keep them out. As I braked and jumped from my truck most of the crowd revved up and blew off in different directions. I was only able to stop four of the violators directly in my path. They were cited into court after pleading their case to me unsuccessfully. We wanted to make an impression and with the news coverage the word soon got out. Whether it curtailed the unlawful operations or not I left the violators with the advice I had been waiting to use.

I warned them to let their fleeing buddies know there was going to be no warnings issued. I told them to tell their friends, "They had better be careful; there's a new Sheriff in town!"

Bill used the quote in his news story and I got a little hazing from my compatriots. I had the feeling the Superiors were not too impressed either but I couldn't resist the opportunity.

I was able to work at that job for several years even after cancer surgery but gradually the toll on the body became too much. I was being frustrated at each turn. The final straw involved the illegal shooting and waste of several cow elk on a hillside off Columbia River Mainline above Clatskanie. Two able bodied loggers and one young Trooper and I went to the scene. We had to go down a steep embankment to a stream, cross the stream and climb perhaps a hundred yards or more up another steep embankment to the animals. With all good intentions I followed along. They easily outpaced me and when I got to the stream I knew I could not make it without some kind of assistance. It was probably the first time in some 40 years that I had to resign myself to the fact I could no longer physically do the job. I was angry and concerned about my helplessness. I yelled at the others that I would be heading back to the road and began the climb out. Luckily there were old skid trails crisscrossing the area and I was able to work my way to the top and slump into my truck. I knew it was over for me. In a way it was a relief but it was definitely a signal that I had entered into a phase in my life that I had never even considered or looked forward to.

Later I was later privileged to be asked by the Superintendent to come to the Legislature in Salem and testify before the Ways and Means Committee for the need to retain Wildlife Officers. My wife and I sat through hours of testimony by various groups asking for funding and when my turn finally came I wadded up my prepared testimony and tossed it aside to speak from the heart.

I told them how I had come to Salem that day nearly 40 years from the time I first was hired. I stopped by the OSP supply office and turned in my uniforms, badges and other issued gear for the last time. I also told them I was working a few nights back and had just finished writing some notes in my notebook at 2:00AM on the hill above Deer Island and was preparing to head for home a couple miles away. A young man came up behind me in his truck, jumped out and began beating on my truck bad crying hysterically. He said a group of intoxicated men several miles up the road had blocked his path, fired several shots and threatened to kill him! I calmed him down and we checked his rig for bullet holes, finding none. I took information to contact him later, released him to go and called Dispatch for backup. Dispatch advised there was no backup of any kind! The old man was it! By now the Members of the Ways and Means Committee were leaning forward and looking a little more interested in what I had to say. I told them I had thoughts of reaching over, turning off my radio and just going home! But I couldn't do it. Here

I was, 68 years old, no longer in the prime of life and I was the only law enforcement in the County?

The testimony concluded with me heading toward the group, picking up backup from Vernonia PD, 25 miles away and OSP Sgt. Larry Lucas coming from his home. By the time we arrived at the spot of the incident all that remained was empty beer cans and spent cartridges. The perps were long gone and probably better so.

My point was; did we really want to leave these Wildlife Officers, often the only Law Enforcement in the outer fringes to fend for themselves? As good as the job was, and as important it was to have them out there the risks were becoming too high. Either make the commitment and fund the positions or deal with the consequences, whatever they night be.

CHAPTER VIII
The coming of the Union

When I was stationed in Beaverton early in my career there was strong union talk due to some perceived and real inequities. I had a strong sense of loyalty to the Department and tried to keep at arms length as good friends were on both sides of the issue. I had a serious resentment of unions probably passed on from my Dad after I saw how union goons in the 1940s had cost him a trucking business he had spent most of his life developing.

An ugly incident that shook the office occurred while I was a young Trooper. "The Committee" an anonymous entity owned by no one in particular made itself known and began demanding justice in disciplinary proceedings. Notes were left taped to lockers initially then tape recordings were sent to the Governor's office. We had one patrol meeting with our "fire breathing" District Captain who slammed his fist so hard on the table, a set of Elk horns hanging on the wall came crashing down and stuck in the leather couch in the squad room. His neck veins were bulging as he demanded to know who was behind "The Committee". No one uttered a word. No one knew. Unbeknownst to the Captain, one of the Troopers secretly recorded the meeting and sent the recording to the Governor's office in Salem. Things spun badly out of control as threats and rumors flew. No one was able to stop the runaway train!

After some serious adjustments things finally settled back to a more normal pace. The Captain summoned several of us to his office and individually confided in us, his desire to see things through. He expressed his confidence in several of us but I could not tell him what I didn't know. To this day no one has admitted to being behind the "Committee". Years later when some of us who were there meet, the "committee" word is dropped. We nod our heads in acknowledgement, but no one will claim to having been part of it. We considered ourselves part of the "survivors" of one of the rougher times in our careers. Nothing could be taken for granted.

Several years later, Holly Holcomb was assassinated on the steps to the Public Service building where he had worked for so many years. He was a good and fair man who deserved to live out his life. A disgruntled former employee was responsible and convicted of the crime.

One of the things I leaned early on with the Department was to avoid irritating superiors. If you screwed up, take ownership, come clean and all was usually forgotten. "Now get your ass back out on the road!" Like it never happened.

One very busy night, a car was left parked in the middle of Canyon Road with no one around. Just before Christmas traffic was medium to heavy and I had the car towed. I thought it had been logged, but it was my responsibility and I forgot to do the necessary paperwork. Several months later the tow company filed the lien on the car. The owner had reported it stolen after he left it parked in the middle of the highway. Fortunately for me all parties agreed to drop any charges and the car was returned. All I could do was apologize and the matter was dropped.

I began my career in the Fish and Wildlife Division and in the first year as a Wildlife Officer, my partner and I ran afoul of the Wildlife Lieutenant. He was apparently on a misguided mission when he came to the office, called us in to review our first year stats and proclaimed we were "fired". We were quite shocked by the abrupt manner of this guy and fortunately our immediate Commander and Station Lieutenant had the presence of mind to tell him to back off, in so many words, and he left in a huff.

We were still in a state of "what the hell happened?" when a District Wildlife Meeting occurred that next week. We arrived at the meeting along with all the Wildlife Officers from the District and were quite taken aback when Major Hershey announced there was a small issue of an apology due to a couple of men in the room. Bob and I sat there as the Lieutenant publicly apologized to us for what he termed an over reaction. It felt as if a great weight was lifted as this rarely happened in a top down Para military organization. My respect for the Department increased greatly that day. We were never again bothered there by overzealous managers and shortly I was offered the position of Commercial Fish Enforcement at St. Helens. I had good rapport with Supervisors and Administrators and three years later I was promoted to Corporal at The Dalles.

Yearly evaluations were contentious at times. I had conference sessions with Commanders regarding the excess, or lack of, hours Troopers worked for the Department, with no compensation of any kind. It was called love time. Most of the men did not object to working "love time", in fact some of them preferred to, but some Administrators felt it was proper for first line supervisors to evaluate them on the number of excess hours. I disagreed. We had always been told excess hours would be looked upon kindly by the Legislature when setting budgets and pay raises. I had a long talk with one of the more understanding Captains from headquarters about this and while he questioned my take on the process he reluctantly agreed that I might be right.

Shortly after that the members of the Department voted in a Union that exists today. The Sergeants were all called to a special meeting with the Superintendent and told we were responsible for the Union vote passing. Did anyone think we could have prevented it?

I watched several disciplinary proceedings under the new union rules involving people who were in our unit. The procedures were long drawn out affairs that surely must have taxed the patience and minds of those who were under scrutiny. I thought back to the old ways when we would walk into the Commander's office and say, "Sir, I screwed up, I'm sorry." These practices were most likely a holdover from military days. I had been a Team Sergeant in an Air Force Engineering Squadron and that was the way it worked, most of the time.

They would reply, "Get out of here and go back to work."

Of course it didn't happen that way all the time. And most likely it will never be that way again.

Norm Minnick, the Last of the Wardens

Sometimes out of forgetfulness, sometimes out of maybe a sense of historical perspective I refer to Wildlife Officers of the Oregon State Police as "Wardens". In a way we were but officially we were Wildlife Officers.

One of the old timers Bob Lund and I worked with on Sauvie Island in our early years was Norm Minnick, a crusty old throwback, (and I say that in a kind way) and one of the last of the old

Wardens who worked directly for Oregon Department of Fish and Wildlife. At that time it was the Oregon Department of Fish and Game and the Oregon Department of Fisheries although they were under one roof.

Norm lived on Sauvie Island in one of the houses owned by the Department and knew the island like the back of his hand. He carried a 45 Automatic on his hip and a silver badge. He wrote tickets when he had to and handled most any enforcement problem in his own gruff, tough way, yet had an extreme amount of patience. When the patience grew thin the temper came out and a slew of expletives flew forth at anyone unfortunate enough to cross him at that moment. Of course we were never allowed the luxury of losing it at less than cooperative violators but Norm would while we stood back and watched the fire fly.

Norm knew more of what went on at times than he let on but what he gave us was more than we could get without his help. Certain things were left handled by "Norm's law". This was confirmed years later either by the perpetrators themselves or by someone else who knew the inside scoop. Old law enforcement was handled that way and it often worked out for the better.

Forty plus years after I worked the Island, another story came to light. I had forgotten about it as no information ever came out pointing to anyone. Near the Eastside check station on the Wildlife Management area is a small boat harbor called Willow Bar. The river had formed a natural slough at right angles to the current and someone at some time had developed a marina there. More than few chases on the river at night culminated in that area with boats simply disappearing into the inlet. If the boat was not identifiable it was simply lost in the mix of other boats or it slipped up the slough into the tangle of Willows that stretched for hundreds of yards.

I was talking to a group of people one day and as we reminisced we discovered we had both known Norm and had a great time telling stories about him. One of the men was talking about Willow Bar and commercial fishermen who used the marina to conduct their legal and sometimes not so legal business of catching fish and bringing them back to share among the small community.

Sturgeon were plentiful in those days with a three fish daily limit and a large size slot limit. Anything between 3 and 6 feet in length could be retained for sport use. And they were considered a nuisance to the netters, as the small ones would tangle and plug their nets and the big ones would tear the net to shreds. Little thought was given to preservation of a creature that had survived since the age of dinosaurs. They were considered plentiful, hard to kill and good to eat; A combination that would lead later to their near demise. The fishermen would bring the Sturgeon that did not fit in the commercial slot limit, which at the time was 4 to 6 feet, and give those fish away to the locals or passing tugboats. It seemed to be a good deal at the time, albeit illegal as hell!

The man told me that one morning the fisherman came in with a huge fish he estimated to be 12 feet long. They struggled to get it off the boat without arousing too much attention. A fish like that would arouse anyone's attention and the fact it was illegal would attract the attention of Law Enforcement, namely us. He told me how they got it in the back of his pickup and he headed out to dispose of the evidence. ODFW had a pit in one of the fields where dead animals of all sorts were disposed of. Road kill deer down to road kill possums, dead waterfowl. Everything went into the pit and was covered over with a bulldozer. Department of Environmental Quality found out about the pit and ordered it closed. ODFW waited a few weeks and opened a new pit. I remembered that part of the story. He told me he drove to the new pit, cut the head and tail off the huge fish, gutted it and left all the disposable parts there in the pit.

Apparently Norm went to the pit to dispose of more carcasses and then discovered the huge Sturgeon head and body parts. It didn't take a rocket scientist to figure out what had occurred and what would happen if Law Enforcement found out about it. It would eventually get back to DEQ and lead to possible serious recriminations for ODFW. As I vaguely recall, some time later, Norm reluctantly mentioned it to us, not wanting to instigate an investigation that would involve a number of people, the re-opening of the pit and the consequences to Department of Fish and Wildlife. It was filed away as a piece of information that would later enable us to put some illegal fishermen completely out of business.

I didn't know to this day, the initial part of the story. Now as a former LEO I'm learning the suspicions we had were valid and not just some barroom talk. Many times we used information that was simply not good enough to build a case on to place fear in the poachers. While they may have thought we had sufficient information to charge them, we actually didn't but would let information slip out and play on their minds. Prevention was the name of the game and if we could prevent the illegal taking of wildlife, that was more productive than catching and prosecuting them after the wildlife was killed. It was a balancing act at best.

We never worked alone on the Island as long as Norm was around. A stop at his home for coffee at night and he would put on his boots, hop in the truck and accompany us on the lonesome night patrols. His stories would fill a book. I just wish I could remember some of them. We never failed to invite Norm to our gatherings and he would sit in the corner with the wives surrounding him regaling them with tales of old! He loved the attention.

I really don't know the history of Department of Fish and Game Wardens other than the fact there were a few around the

State as late as the early 70s. The wildlife enforcement responsibility had actually been handed to the Oregon State Police when they were organized in 1931. The Department of Fisheries was combined with the Department of Fish and Game and became the Department of Fish and Wildlife in 1975.

I was assigned one of the Commercial Fish positions at St. Helens prior to that and often used the guidance and knowledge of another of the old timers from the now defunct Fish Commission. Whenever a problem in Commercial fish law came up I called Elmer Case. Elmer always had time to discuss the in and outs of the Commercial Fishery. It was complicated law, much different than sport fishing laws. Commercial fishermen were regulated by rules that dictated how fish were to be caught, where they could be taken and stored and how they differed from sport caught fish. Often the two ended up in the same place causing minor or not so minor problems.

Bob Lund, Leryl Brown and I had been working for some time on particular individual fishermen who had little regard for commercial seasons and many outlets to dispose of illegally caught fish. Just about any trick that could be used they tried. We learned the record keeping rules required of businesses that dealt in fish. We learned certain fishing techniques that, while they appeared to be legal, were in fact banned practices. These included using large amounts of lead on the lead lines of gillnets in shallow water so the nets would "set" all night in one spot and load up with little or no effort on the part of the fishermen. Armed with the information from Elmer we used citations and arrest to stop the illegal activity.

While my superiors chafed at the practice of using ODFW employees to explain the law, it was helpful to us and enabled us to keep current. Elmer also fed information that we normally would not get from ODFW managers for fear it would alienate the commercial fishermen and cause them to hold back information they needed. It always seemed strange to me that we were expected to overlook small violations in the Commercial industry that regularly brought huge fines and suspensions in the Sport industry. More than once it was hinted that we were putting a little too much pressure on the commercial fishery and it could possibly harm the relationship of Commercial fishermen to the Biologists gathering the data they needed. I filed it in the back of my mind and kept on doing what I felt I was being paid to do. Enforce the law!

Another true "character" I met recently is a retired Master Chief Petty Officer Bob Gedlick of the U.S Coast Guard. I have always had the highest admiration for this agency and the work they performed, not just saving lives, but the role they took on saving wildlife. I spent more than a few days working on U.S. Coast Guard Fishery patrol boats up and down the Pacific Ocean off Oregon.

The Chief retired well before I came on the Department, but related some great stories from Ports such as Newport, Tillamook Bay and Rogue River. We never bothered checking the Coast Guard Life boats that would spend all day on the water at the mouths of the bays shepherding the sport fishing fleet. They usually brought their sport gear along and joined in the fishing activity, but would quickly drop everything and run to aid boats in distress. New Officers would occasionally check them for licenses and gear and we tactfully asked them to ignore minor violations. These guys were out here to save lives and a little trade off seemed to be proper.

Like normal red blooded men and women they liked to unwind at the local tavern after duty. Most of the taverns and bars had good food and fresh fish on the menu. The thought crossed someone's mind that all that fresh fish they were catching might be traded for cold beer at the tavern. So it was worked out with a few places to bring in fresh salmon to trade for free beer. While on the surface it seemed innocent enough, there were commercial fishermen whose livelihood depended on selling their catch locally. So the problem reared up and according to the Chief, one of the State Police Wildlife Officers paid him a visit and explained the problem that had developed. Too many Salmon were entering the restaurant bar trade and the commercial people were becoming annoyed. The Chief assured the Wildlife Officer that the problem would be taken care of. It was.

I have spent more than a few hours listening to fascinating stories that occurred before my time on the Department. Chief showed me some original paperwork he had submitted to the Coast Guard in Washington D.C. that suggested the use of the highly visible and recognized orange slash on the hulls of all U.S Coast Guard vessels, large and small. It was adopted but the credit went to then President John F. Kennedy. Like any good military man, Bob just shrugged his shoulders and put the paperwork back into his file.

Chief was also responsible for the redesign of cockpits on the smaller patrol boats. Open cockpits allowed the "Cox" to see what was happening in a rescue but often resulted in "green water" smacking the operator full in the chest and face knocking them senseless. After a day on the water and taking a couple of waves over the top, Chief described the feeling of having been in a prize fight. The newer cockpits deflect the water around the Cox and still allow for visibility.

The older son of one of our friends, Terry Vanderwerf, has risen to Command Master Chief of the Coast Guard. Terry used to fish with his Dad and me off the coast near Astoria when our boys were all youngsters. Terry visited home recently and I asked him if he would come and meet Master Chief Gedlick. When I introduced them the old Chief's eyes lit up and the stories started flying. Two hours later they were still trying to outdo each other... No one can tell stories like Coast Guard Chiefs!

Problematic Rex

I always felt just a little fortunate to have met Rex when I did, several years after I retired. I have the funny feeling he could have been one of my problematic customers had I met him while I was still working. We were into our fourth year of business in Alaska and I got a phone call early on before the season had actually begun.

"Hey this is Rex and I want the same room we had last year, OK?"

I was just a little puzzled because I didn't know anyone named Rex, but I strung it along. "Ok which room did you have?"

"You know the one down on the end away from the loud music." He replied.

Then it hit me. We were often mistaken for the hotel up the road that had a similar name. I figured this one sounded too good to pass up.

"I'll tell you what Rex. All of our rooms are quiet and what's more we have a view. How about fishing? Do you have that taken care of already?" I was selling him on our place as fast as I could before he realized his mistake and hung up.

"You know what, I like your style." he replied. "I think we'll stay with you guys this year."

"Welcome to Clam Gulch Lodge." I said not even dreaming what lay ahead.

A few months later at the peak of the Salmon season Rex and his wife Jackie arrived at the Lodge. Both were loveable and friendly people and ready to go fishing. I was having a good streak on the Kenai and another couple was booked for the next day. Rex showed me his gear, new rods and reels, and assured he knew "what the hell he was doing" having been a guide himself.

That should have scared me a bit but it didn't. I tried to convince him to use my equipment but he persisted.

We hit the river early and went straight for the lower end to catch the tide. Back trolling plugs was the order of the day as it had been several days before. We were using Sardine oil liberally on everything including the floor of the boat. I cautioned the clients to stay seated and watch their step and I was well aware of the slick wet floors, oil or not.

Jackie's rod slammed down and the drag was screaming as a big Kenai King headed downriver. I grabbed the net and stood up to alert the other boats that we had one on. About that time, Jackie's reel fell off! Remember the brand new rods and Rex's admonishment that he had "been a guide"? By the time I reattached the reel to the pulsating rod the fish got off and we all sat back down.

"Now, do you want to use my gear, or not?" I asked.

It was agreed to use mine and we settled back into the seats. A few minutes later, Jackie's rod went down again and this time my reel stayed on my rod. She's doing a great job on the fish and just as she gets it under control, I get the boat away from the crowd and into the middle of the river. Everything is working like it should. At this point Rex jumps up and announces he'll net the fish, something I seldom allowed, but Rex was a "guide".

Rex waits till Jackie skillfully brings the fish alongside, and then makes his move. The fish is in the net! Rex is overboard in the water, head first!

"Keep calm everyone I have it under control" I muttered. I had Rex by the belt and with the aid of Gordon we hoisted him spitting and sputtering back into the boat.

But the net is empty, the fish is gone and Rex is soaked. I'm pissed, confused, a little bit scared and trying to sort things out. Fortunately none of the other boats in the area even saw what happened. What the hell happened? At this point I looked at Gordon, a very polite gentleman who had fished with me several times and he mimed putting a bottle to his lips and pointed at Rex.

"Rex, have you been drinking?" I asked. Drinking was a definite negative in my boat on this river.

"Well yeah, I always drink when I go fishing." Rex replied sheepishly.

We finished out the day fishless and I was not in a good mood when we got to the Lodge. I explained everything to my wife who calmly assured me it would be better tomorrow.

"There's not going to be a tomorrow for him." I snapped, "I could have lost my license or worse he could have died! No one drinks in my boat on that river."

Jackie and Rex came down from their room and were joking about the day's events. I warmed up to their charm and finally agreed to take them out on the river one more time, on the condition that there would be no alcohol.

The next morning was a beautiful day as we headed to the river with another couple from the lodge. I saw Rex pull off at a convenience store and when we got to the boat ramp I waited. He pulled in and I met him in the lot. I shook him down and found another bottle under his coat.

"Thanks Rex, we'll all have a drink after we go fishing." I told him as I placed it in my truck and locked the door.

"You are one serious SOB." He winked as we climbed in the boat.

It was a beautiful day we limited the boat with great fish and got some of the best pictures in the five years I guided up there. And I made a friend for life. Can it get any better than that?

When I got back to Oregon I had quite a few fishing adventures with Rex before he passed away suddenly of cancer a few years ago. He could be one ornery character when he was drinking but had a heart of gold inside. One trip that stood out from the others was the day we were bobber fishing for Chinook in Trask River tidewater. Rex was good at it and hooked a beauty of a chrome hen, bonked her and started fishing again.

"You are going to tag that fish Rex? I asked.

"Hell no, I never tag fish." He replied knowing it would elicit a little of the old Law Officer in me. "If you want to tag it, you tag it."

"You know I won't do that, give me your tag." I shot back.

He tossed me his harvest card and when I looked at it I could see it was clean. No entries! I knew he had taken several fish earlier in the year so I just guessed at the dates and filled it in. He looked at me incredulous that I had used up his spaces on his tag as I filled in the last one he had just caught.

"Damn you! You never stop being a cop do you?" he started laughing.

I had one on him. But I don't think I got the last laugh. Not long before the last time I saw Rex alive, he was camping at Jetty Fishery and I was staying at Paradise Cove doing dock checks part time with OSP. I pulled into the camp ground early in the morning, the tide was low and a small pool of water was left behind the jetty. Rex was standing there with his salmon rod, soaking wet holding a 25 pound chrome bright fish. His story, and somehow I didn't believe it, was that he woke up and saw the fish splashing in the pool. He cast his spinner and the fish bit pulling him off his feet and into the water before he could control it. He swore it was true. I had seen one other fish jerk him into the water a few years back. There were no witnesses! I made sure he tagged the fish. Rest in peace Rex! I'll never forget you.

Cases gone awry

When I initially began working in the Wildlife division it was pretty obvious to all there were laws and procedures that historically had been used to build cases but were in fact flawed and relatively useless. Periodically we would to court and lose good cases mainly because we followed flawed regulations. When it was pointed out, the Administrators would advise to go easy, when in fact the proper course would have been to change the regulations to conform to constitutional law.

In other instances there were solid laws based on following good procedure that had simply never been tested in court. One instance was the power to inspect, on a random basis, commercial establishments that dealt in wildlife products. Random meant exactly that, not based on prior information or probable cause because in those cases it would be necessary to obtain a search warrant, show exigent circumstances or obtain permission to search.

Commercial fish receiving stations and custom packing houses were prevalent on the river and it was simply good patrol technique to regularly stop by and inspect records and stock on hand. While some of these places did their best to discourage the checks, others welcomed them. Often the managers themselves were no more than employees but were still responsible for the records and stock. They did not want to be caught with illegal or out of date records.

In a case that solidified the question of commercial establishment's expectation of privacy or lack thereof, a case wound its way to the Oregon State Court of Appeals. Westside Fish, a small processor, wholesaler, custom packer operated just outside Rainier, Oregon. We periodically and on a random basis checked the product and records and periodically found violations that were cited into court. I don't recall how many cases were involved but eventually the business owners put up signs in the yard and demanded they be left alone. We persisted until the case was taken to the Court of Appeals. In a ruling the Court basically said that random checks were not only legal but expected under the law and if persons elected to engage in a pervasively regulated business they could expect to be pervasively regulated.

In another case, the practice of holding road checks existed statewide during hunting seasons and at times during fishing seasons. Hunters, for the most part, consented, approved and expected the checks that were meant to deter violators and also gather biological information. Several incidents occurred when people refused to allow searches of their vehicles. Eager Officers pushed the point and refused to allow the hunter to continue on without being checked. The State was sued and rather than fight they agreed to pay civil penalties to the parties. Eventually the State Attorney General ruled against any form of road checks claiming they were violating the constitutional rights of citizens. Most of us believed it would have been wiser to fight the individual cases and retain the checks as other States had done successfully.

I had occasion to experience the "new way" when I was working contract as a Wildlife Officer out of Tillamook checking the local docks. I was at Nehalem Bay when a fisherman told me about a 55 pound Salmon that had been caught nearby. It was already on one of the private docks at a local motel and I wanted to see it. 55 pound Salmon are not caught often here. I walked to the dock and down the gangway to where the proud fishermen were. I congratulated them on their catch and the lucky angler wanted to show me his tag. I looked at it and thanked him again and was not so politely greeted with, "Who invited you down here?"

I turned and faced a very serious lady who appeared to be not happy with my presence. I responded that I had just come down to look at the fish.

"You are not welcome here at any time without permission." She advised.

I left and later that day reported the incident to the Sergeant in charge. Brent laughed and told me the Officers referred to that as "Schwab's law" after an incident that occurred when two Officers entered a boathouse without permission to check some ducks. I was the unfortunate Supervisor at the time that had to take minor disciplinary action on the incident. The hunter who owned the boathouse called me at Headquarters and told me of the incident. He and his friend had been hunting near Aldrich Point and were returning to their boathouse where they were staying. They entered from the river side and were tying their boat when two Officers walked in on them from the house. He explained that he had living quarters at the boathouse and the only way in was through the house. He was merely looking for an apology as he felt his rights had been violated. I told him I would look into the case and get back to him. After interviewing the two Officers, they insisted they were under the impression that the structure was not a dwelling. From the citizen's description and their description I concluded it was a dwelling.

I contacted the Lieutenant to advise him of the problem. It was determined by all the Command that some rights were violated and training was in order. We conducted several days of training on search and seizure rules. Basically the Officers had violated the tenets of search and seizure. Fortunately the owner was a reasonable man and declined to push the case. Procedure was spelled out and if that came as result of my actions, I'll take full credit. I firmly believed in the rules and procedures and adherence to the rights of the people.

This policy has been expanded upon to now exclude any Wildlife Officer from entering private property to merely check hunting licenses or equipment. I wonder how anyone can enforce laws designed to protect wildlife.

An administrative rule once existed that vaguely suggested a Wildlife Officer, in the exercise of enforcing Wildlife laws, could search outbuildings or containers they suspected had illegal game. When tested this rule was found to be patently unconstitutional but it took some years to wind its way out of practice and caused several Officers to suffer investigations into their conduct when they were following what they thought was legal procedure.

The practical side of Wildlife Law Enforcement puts an Officer working with little or no backup in remote areas, contacting armed hunters and often survivalists with the mentalities of people like Claude Dallas who intentionally killed two Idaho Wildlife Officers who were simply doing their job.

I have talked to dozens of Police Officers who worked the roughest parts of major cities, gang areas and outlying areas, but cringed at the very thought of overtaking vehicles alone in the middle of nowhere, knowing the occupants were most likely armed.

Defensive tactics instructors often just shook their heads at the scenarios they heard during in-service training describing the vehicle stop tactics Wildlife Officers employed in the deep dark woods.

Yes there were times, walking up to a car load of armed hunters, that suddenly the hair stood up on the back of my neck as it sunk in that maybe I had stretched beyond my limitations and placed myself in a really hazardous situation. The senses become very focused and training kicks in. Most of the time the Wildlife Officer walks away and continues on his patrol. I would guess that looking back on events long after they happened make them seem more dicey then they really were.

I recall one night long ago when I came into the office after my shift and saw a young Trooper preparing for patrol. He was sitting at the table, hands folded, and a very serious expression on his face. I asked if anything was wrong. He replied that he was just "psyching up" for his patrol. He confided that he was extremely worried most of the time for his safety. I suggested that maybe he was not cut out for this kind of work. We talked a bit about the job and the training we had received. I felt strongly that one had to love the job and all it entailed in order to get the most out of it. While none of us were overconfident or even gung ho, we were secure that our training had adequately prepared us to face the situation. I don't know what ever happened to the Trooper but I believe he left the Department some time later.

My wife and I meet regularly with Tim and Gail Mansfield for dinner out. Tim was with me the night I got hit on the freeway. He said the incident left him with bad memories to this day. I was lucky and remember nothing. We talk about the days when it was expected that we mitigated cases in the field. Everything did not have to come before a judge or jury. The Police Officer many times handed out street justice and sent the parties on their ways. Family disputes, even the ones involving weapons, were answered by one or maybe two Officers. Incarceration was the last resort. It wasn't that we were braver, wiser, more daring or tougher it was just the way things were done at the time.

I used to ask my wife if she was worried when I was working especially at night. She said of course she worried but she knew it was what I wanted to do and she was sure I would not take any unnecessary chances. I always came home!

USFWS presence

Early on in the 70s USFWS became a bigger part of the enforcement scene. Again many of the older Administrators had experienced less than desirable performance from the Agents of that Agency. However our experience was always good, from Agents who worked from dawn to dusk, taking any task we asked of them and accompanying on the long river patrols. Soon they were equipped with modern devices and nicer boats than we had and willingly shared them.

I can't imagine how we could have accomplished the Commercial assignments and waterfowl season without their help through the 90s. NMFS Agents followed suit and soon became a powerful force on the Tribal fisheries and the huge Offshore Fisheries. Their expertise came from former careers with OSP, WDFW, Idaho Fish and Game and many other Law Enforcement Agencies across the US. In fact they began picking off the cream of the crop causing some angst among the Department heads. I benefited from the transfer of one Officer to NMFS when the opening occurred at St. Helens. Shortly after that I was considered from a NMFS job in Kodiak Alaska. My family was not enthused about it and we decided to remain with the Department.

I still remain friends with many of the Agents. Earl Kisler, Ed Wickersham, Wayne Lewis, Jerry Woods, Dean Owren, Dave McMullen, Rod Moxley. Out of respect to them I will decline to tell stories about them as they could easily tell some about me.

One book I would highly recommend is "Sea Cop" by Wayne Lewis. It is a masterful work of chronicling the high seas fishery and work by the Agents of NMFS. It is exciting and intense reading with cloak and dagger episodes involving foreign agents.

Hunting the wrong season

One of the stranger cases I was involved in came one afternoon in the late fall of the 1980s while I was in The Dalles. Sr. Trooper Mike DeBolt called me and advised he had stopped a rig for a minor violation on I 84 coming back from hunting cow season east of the mountains. A man, his wife and teenage son had all been successful tagging three antlerless Elk. The elk were all hanging in quarters from the side racks of the trailer. No attempt to cover them up or other wise conceal them were made.

Mike had no reason to suspect anything was wrong and asked to see their tags for the elk.

The man was very cooperative and happy with their successful hunt. Upon inspection of the tags it was determined they were valid for the second season which had not started yet. When Mike showed the tags to the man he expressed surprise and insisted he had applied for first season as he had done for many years. His openness and candor was enough to convince Mike that there perhaps had been some kind of mistake. He took all the information and sent the man and his family on his way west.

Mike returned to the office, contacted Fish and Wildlife in Portland and gave them the information he had. They researched the applications and found the one in question, filled out properly for the second season in the man's own handwriting. Now there was no doubt of a violation so Mike called me at The Dalles and advised me of the situation. I went out to the freeway and stopped the rig as they came through The Dalles. I explained the situation and asked them to follow me to the State Police office located just off the freeway.

When we arrived I explained the situation to the man and advised him that he had indeed applied for second season tags. He was insistent and demanded to go before a Judge immediately. I called the local District Attorney and asked him if that would be possible as the man did not want to come back to The Dalles from Portland. Bernie Smith checked with the District Judge and advised me it was permissible to bring the man over.

He was advised of his right to have an attorney present to represent him but declined, just wanting to get it over with and be on his way.

The Judge heard our testimony in the case and was shown the documents possessed by the hunters. The man had left his wife and son at the office as they were not cited in accordance with Department policy.

After the State presented its case the man testified that he had applied for the first season and that was all he had to say. I fully expected the Judge to fine the man and send him on his way. What happened then was surprising to me and to the defendant. The Judge pronounced him "guilty of a horrible mistake" and fined him $1500 and 10 days in jail to be served immediately.

The defendant began to protest and lost his voice at which time the Judge advised me to take him out before he said something that would cost him even more time in jail. I asked the Judge what the disposition of the animals would be. He advised me the animals were to be seized and donated to charitable institutions. By this time the defendant was getting extremely agitated as I led him out of the Courtroom. Out in the hall he nearly collapsed in anger and was turned over to the County Jailers.

Somewhat perplexed by the severity of the sentence I returned to the Office and contacted the man's wife and son, explained what happened and that I would be taking the illegal Elk. The teenage son started screaming at me and jumped up on the trailer, removed the quarters of Elk and began tossing them onto the ground. I had remained patient through most of this but finally had enough. I sharply told him if he did not calm down I could probably arrange to have him stay in detention. I explained the entire episode could have been avoided had the defendant simply checked his application and return tags. In no way was there any responsibility on my part, Sr. Trooper DeBolt's part or the Judge's part to rectify what the Judge properly called a "horrible mistake".

Years later I had the opportunity to discuss the case with one of the other Judges who had risen to U.S. Court of Appeals. He and I both agreed it was one of those catch 22 situations that had no good outcome. The defendant had never taken any responsibility other than "I thought". I took no pleasure from the case but could never come up with an alternative solution. And it was probably one of those instances that required consulting with an Attorney.

Fishing With Jimmy

Probably one of the more memorable assignments I had toward the end of my career was accompanying President Jimmy Carter on a fishing trip on the Willamette River. Lt. Dudley Nelson, my immediate Supervisor set up the trip upon request. President Carter was long retired in 1993 when this took place. But it was still an honor and a privilege. He was visiting with a local Attorney, John Schwabe who co incidentally had been an acquaintance of my Dad years ago. They used to prod each other about whose name was spelled correctly.

We met in the parking lot at the mouth of the Clackamas River and Professional Guide and all around nice guy Steve Kohler was picked to guide "Jimmy" as he preferred to be called. Jimmy was gracious and friendly and my assignment was to take the secret service detail in my boat and fish along with the guide boat dogging them at every twist and turn. Dudley accompanied the President along with Mr. Schwabe.

From the get go I knew I was going to have to pay attention to what I was doing. The Secret Service guys were really cordial and funny to be around, telling jokes and having a great time. They confided how Jimmy liked to fish and they did to, so fish they did.

I had each of them outfitted with Salmon rods and proper bait. We were mostly trolling in the swollen river and not expecting to really catch anything but just pass the time. I would be trolling along with the 7.5 Honda and suddenly Steve would fire the big engine and race out ahead with no warning. We would quickly reel in, hit the throttle on the 200 HP jet and follow as best we could.

Like I said I didn't really expect to hook up but was telling the Agents how it might happen. I told them if we hooked up we could run up alongside the President's boat and hand off the fish to him.

One Agent looked at me with a cocky smile and said, "The hell with Jimmy, let him catch his own fish! I'm not giving up my fish."

I had to laugh at that one. We had a fishless day never the less but just the experience was something I always treasured.

Steve Kohler had volunteered his boat and time for the trip, but one guide who apparently had a burr under his saddle, tried to make an issue of the event. This was just about the time Coast Guard licenses were being required for all guides. Steve had not procured his yet but was donating his time to the event so none was required.

The Coast Guard got word of the trip and contacted our office demanding to know the details of the trip. We politely explained the circumstances and how in our view no laws had been broken. They persisted in calling and demanding reports from us regarding the trip so they could proceed with their "investigation". Nothing we said could satisfy them so the entire correspondence was sent off to President Carter to see if something could be explained at a higher level.

Shortly thereafter we received notice that the Coast Guard was no longer pursuing the investigation.

The only other President who came to Oregon to fish while I was there was George Bush Sr. during his presidency. We got the word he wanted to do a little Steelhead fishing on the Sandy River. It was to be a quick stop, so a guide was contacted to locate the fish. The river was low and clear, not particularly good fishing conditions but a couple of Steelhead were located and the entourage came in. The poor guide was overwhelmed by security and tried his best to put President Bush on the fish. Helicopters circled overhead with Secret Service and Agents prowled the bushes around the river. It was over before it got going and President Bush went on with his business after tossing some flies at the sulking Steelhead.

After I retired I went into the guide and lodging business in Alaska. I sent a note to Carter Headquarters in Georgia, inviting Jimmy to join us on the Kenai River. He was well into Habitat for Humanity at the time and politely declined the offer. I think I could have gotten him into a Salmon or two up there and maybe even some for his Agents.

CHAPTER IX
Typical Patrol Moments

Many of the Officers I talked to over the years have given me stories but were reluctant to create one of their own. I put together bits and pieces of stories I either heard or was involved in and created some stories that I hope will portray the days in the life of the average Wildlife Officer if such a person exists. Remember the stories are real; the characters have been created out of bits and pieces. No resemblance to any Officer living or dead intended. . Here is the story in the Trooper's words.

I'm Ted Arno a sixteen year veteran with OSP working out of the Enterprise Station. I grew up in nearby Baker City, finished high school, went on to a couple of years of Community College when the opportunity came up with the State. My sights were set on working Fish and Wildlife and that is exactly what happened. Most people have no idea what it is like to work each and every day in the remote parts of the State, either packing into remote areas by horseback, running whitewater river in jet boats or rafts and 4 wheeling off the main roads into areas seen only by occasional hunters and cowboys.

I am 6 years into my second marriage. The job is of utmost importance and the lack of a regular schedule, the oft times call outs in the middle of the night, staying at the job till it was finished all contribute to the difficulty of maintaining normal family relations.

I have a pretty good working relationship with the locals and they know me as a no nonsense yet sociable friend. I know they are my best source of information and they know I would never cross them or disclose any confidential information they give to me. It has to work that way. Trust is all that there was in the remote backcountry.

My "normal day" consists of checking all of my equipment, reading the desk log for any information logged by other Troopers that might be of value or interest to my daily patrols. I never run the same route, the same way more than twice a month. People here are used to routines and if they ever figured out a Wildlife Officer's patrol habits they could easily take advantage of it and feed off it

I decide to head north on the rim road around the North Powder, check out some of the smaller logging roads between there and Sumpter and work my way down to Dixie Summit. Some of the old gold mining claims are still active in there and prospectors have a habit of living off the land if they can get away with it. It's late July and hunting season is still a month away.

My old Dodge 4x4 has plenty of miles on it but is as reliable as an old horse. And all I have to do at night is park it and it's ready to go in the morning. Extra 40 gallon fuel tanks in the bed provided several days fuel. I settled in the well worn seat, turned on the local news station and signed in on duty with Dispatch.

They would track my movements thru my shift by radio checks on the hour. I had the option to go off the grid for longer periods of time if I wanted. The day settled in to be rather normal. A couple of trout fishermen at the reservoir, mushroom hunters in the higher Pines and some varmint hunters looking for sage rats, the scourge of the cattlemen.

The little rats bred year round and dug big deep holes that could break the leg of a cow that might step in it. Shooting rats was a popular sport among hunters and ranchers wanting to tune their skills. A three inch rat at 100 yards was a formidable target. All it took was a scoped small caliber rifle, lots of ammo and a shooting bench in a strategic location and it was game on!

At the top of the priority list for Wildlife Officers assigned to the area were the trophy Deer, Elk, Antelope and Bighorn Sheep that roamed the hills. These animals did not get big by being stupid or visible, even in the off seasons. My partner, Tom Ahock, and I had to rely on the local Biologists to follow the movements of the animals, especially the Bighorns who would wander miles from their home range. Unscrupulous outlaws and sometimes lowlife vandals shot and killed trophies just so they could brag about it to their equally challenged friends. These were often the hardest cases to crack, no motive, no utilization of the parts, only the inability of the guilty parties to keep from bragging about what great shots they were. Ballistic evidence proved the undoing of more than one of these type poachers. Talking cases required a great deal of sleuthing, physical evidence and then getting down to the talk, trying to convince the suspect we had more than enough evidence and how it would be to their benefit if they just came clean.

I pushed the Dodge over several bad spots in the back road network and finally began the descent to more level roads and smoother sailing. A ranch ahead was on my list to glean for information. Two old brothers had lived there forever and got along quite well. One had assumed the outdoor duties, tending the small herd of mangy Herefords, a small herd of goats and two donkeys. The other one took care of the house, grounds and cooking. He was quite good at whipping up a berry cobbler, or shepherd's pie. He reached his limit though at anything that resembled fresh meat on a bun or steak and mashed potatoes. These concoctions came out greasy, or burnt, the only two ways he knew.

I pulled into the driveway and waited while the Australian Shepherd/Dingo dogs checked out my rig. I learned from experience that getting out too quickly might result in a nipped heel or two. Satisfied the dogs had checked my rig thoroughly; I opened the door and stretched my legs. One of the dogs eyed me and looked like he was going to make his move at my ankles. I carried a walking stick of sizeable proportion and tapped it in a way that let the dog know he would get it across his nose if he tried.

Emil came out of the house and greeted me, happy to have someone to talk to besides his brother. "Want some coffee?" he asked.

"Not today Emil." I replied, thinking back to the last time Emil pulled out a dusty cup shook out the dead flies and filled it with coffee. The coffee had a strange film that resembled an oil slick so I pretended to sip at the coffee and when the opportunity arose fed it to the bushes.

The inside of the old farm house was devoid of any comfortable furniture. Several old wooden chairs served as sitting spots and a wooden table caked with who knows what stood in the kitchen. Dead flies were everywhere. Flypaper rolls hung from the ceiling like spiral party favors, having done their function long ago, crusted with flies and moths. Still these old guys lived happily in their surroundings content with their little estate on the banks of the river.

"Had any outsiders lately coming by?" I inquired.

"Just our regular group of varmint hunters." Emil replied. "They were kind enough to bring some fresh salmon over from the coast and some of the elk sausage from their hunt last year. Nice of them to do that for us."

"I hope you have the salmon in the freezer till you cook it." I advised. "It can go bad in a hurry in this weather. You and your brother can eat well for a while."

"Oh yeah, the one thing we have here that works good is the freezer and my Brother Tony!" Emil laughed at his joke.

"Hey Emil, when you gonna' sell me one of those old cars rotting away out there by the barn?" I asked. "I sure would like to restore the old Model A or even one of those post war Chevys."

"Well, I don't think me and Tony would sell any of those. You know they all belonged to a family member and there are just too many memories." Emil went on. "Someday we might want to fix one up again, you never know."

"Right!" I thought, "Those cars will rust into the ground and will never move, but that's the way it is out here."

Collectors were frowned upon in this part of the country, as if they were trying to steal something. It was a funny part of life, stuff that wasn't really worth scrap, being sought after by collectors and hoarded by old timers who would take it to their grave. Then the relatives moved in and sold it all to a scrap dealer to get rid of it fast.

Tony came up to the house from the barn where he had been working on an old trailer, getting it ready for the last of the hay season. Getting the hay into the barn was utmost importance even though the barn had two foot holes in the roof. It would last a few more years.

"How you doing Ted?" Tony asked.

Before I could answer, Tony was going off on the local Fish and Wildlife guys who "didn't know a damn thing about managing Elk or Deer herds and if they just listened to good cattle ranchers, who did this for a real living, they would learn."

I laughed at Tony and pointed my stick at the scrawny herd of cows munching on alfalfa hay in the corral. "You mean like those?"

Tony knew me well enough to brush it off and threatened not to let me hunt pheasants along the creek if I kept that up.

"Well guys, I got to be getting on down the road. Just wanted to stop and say hi." I said. "Don't go poaching any deer after I leave now."

I decided to go on to Farewell Bend that evening, spend the night at one of the ODFW cabins and work my way back home through the Wallowa Whitman National Forest the next day. Nothing in particular prompted me to go that way but sometimes a diversion from routine can yield results. The only real weapon thinly spread Wildlife officers have is the ability to show up at unexpected times in unexpected places.

I went to the local Burger Shack, ate and shot some pool, then went back to the cabin and signed off for the night. As I laid in the bunk I day dreamed about retirement in 5 or 6 more years. I thought about maybe a little part time job working in a sporting goods store or maybe fishing guide, anything to keep busy. I would have to do something till my kids were out of school. I had saved enough money to help them and hoped they would be ambitious enough to work while they were in school like I did. Growing up in Eastern Oregon taught young men and women the value of hard work. I heard all the problems other Officers had raising kids in the Metro areas of Western Oregon and wanted no part of it for my family. I began to drift off to sleep with the sounds of silence, occasional Owl hoots and a Coyote yelp in the distant hills. I recited an old verse I had written some years ago, about a fictitious Game Warden that lived only in my head. It helped put me to sleep.

Old Red

He was a big hunk of man, Old Red.
Fearing nothing he understood.
Cautious of what he did not
And wary of those he encountered.

His mind was quick and kept him alive
More than once it helped him survive.
All in a days work, his mind told him so
He continued to prosper, his skills to grow.

One night alone on a high mountain top
Red had occasion to make a great stop.
He heard from a distance the sound like a shot
And instantly deduced that something was caught.

He carefully worked his way up the hill
And seriously tested his fine stalking skill.
As he stealthily made his way to the spot
He considered his actions may just be for naught'

His mind was amazed at the sight he did see
A houndsman had made a difficult tree
There in the crotch of an upturned tree root
Was none other than Sasquatch, some call Bigfoot

The houndsman was shaking, holding his gun
And Red was a ponderin', who, what had done
Bigfoot was shakin', his misty eyes glowin'
Wishin' he was out of here, in other words goin'.

Old Red took a deep breath and uttered these word
"Put that gun down you worthless little turd"
As long as I'm boss here no ones going to kill
A creature that means no ill will. Got it Bill?

The houndsman named Bill complied with a sigh
And Bigfoot lit out of there into the nigh'
Bill sniveled and groaned about losing the prize
Old Red just stepped up and said "license please?"

In conclusion this story has only one ending
When you think about rules you want to start bending
Old Red will sneak up and get in your head
You may just as well stayed home in your bed!

I awoke early and was on the road by 6:00AM signed in and feeling good. I wanted to get off the beaten path early so I could spend more time looking for sign and less time looking for errant drivers. Dropping the Dodge into four wheel drive and low range gave me the sense of security. I could pay less attention to the dirt road and more attention to what was off in the brush. If I ran off the road slightly I simply drove back onto the harder surface and continued on. Something off color caught my eye ahead and as I approached I knew it wasn't paper or trash. A tree rat scampered off the object and I stopped to check it out. A piece of gut from an animal was lying on the edge of the road, but no animal was in sight. I noticed blood traces on the brush and drag marks from back in the woods. I slowly worked my way back to a hastily made gut pile. Whoever gutted the animal, most likely a deer, did it quickly and sloppily leaving footprints around the scene and some paper towels they used to wipe their hands.

Back out on the road, I scanned the surface for casings. Two 22 Magnum casings were lying in the middle of the road. The favorite of poachers! I picked them up, looked at the tire tracks and my experience told me it was probably a compact car of some sort, that continued on into the woods. I was determined to run the poachers to ground. I kicked the shifter lever into high range and followed fresh tracks on the dirt road. This was a Wildlife Officer's favorite scenario. Few cars had been down the road; in fact the poachers and I were the only ones that morning as far as I could tell. I knew it was just a matter of time. Less than two miles down the road I saw the tracks veer off on an obvious dead end road. I knew it as a road closure during the regular deer season. No tracks were coming out so I was confident I had the poachers. When I got within a half mile of the end of the road, I blocked the road with my pickup at a place where there was no chance of anything going around and got out with my binoculars and Winchester. One could never be too cautious. It could be some dumb yokels or some really bad ass guys passing through. I walked slowly glassing the road ahead. At about 400 yards I observed the rear end of a small car parked head in where the creek ran near the road. I waited until I saw one of the poachers come back to the car with a plastic bag full of something and place it in the trunk.

The guy then lit a joint and hollered at his buddy to hurry up. "I'm going to smoke all the weed myself if you don't get your ass up here." He laughed.

I was on full alert but confident I had the upper hand. I was not going to let them get in the car if I could help it. The first guy disappeared so I crept silently along the brushy edge of the road till I was within 40 yards of the car. Now I could see the entire car and remain hidden with plenty of cover. I didn't have to wait long as the other poacher, a fat kid, obviously out of shape, with his pants about to fall off stumbled back to the car.

"Gimme some weed," he begged, "I'm tired dragging that damn deer around for you, asshole!"

The other guy, a pimply faced, shaggy haired scruff, just laughed and handed him the joint. They placed the rest of their booty in the trunk and were standing there when I bellowed out in my best commanding voice.

"Hey, you boneheads, put your hands over your head, lace your fingers and face the car now. This is the State Police. One wrong move from either of you and you get a free ride in an ambulance. Understand?"

The two, who had probably less than 40 years on the earth total, were at first stunned, then frightened. The fat one threw his hands up laced his fingers and fell flat on his face. The other one did as he was told and started to speak.

"Quiet!" I ordered. "I do the talking here. When I ask you a question then you can answer. Where are your guns?"

"In the car sir." The skinny one replied, shaking.

By this time I had moved to a position within ten yards of the two and could see everything I needed to see for my safety. The car had Oregon plates but sported a Portland dealer plate frame. One at a time I carefully handcuffed both and quickly searched their pockets for weapons.

"Is anyone else with you?" I asked.

"No just the two of us Officer. Hey you really scared the crap out of us. Are we going to jail?" the fat one asked.

"Probably to post bail." I replied. "Now can I look in your trunk and see what you scoundrels have been up to. How many deer have you killed this morning?"

"Just one. But I guess that's one too many huh? The skinny guy relied.

I asked the kid if I could look in the already unlocked trunk. The kid readily agreed and I lifted the lid and looked at several plastic bags full of boned out deer meat. "I hope you didn't litter the creek with the rest of the carcass and bones."

"No they are all piled on dry ground."

"Well at least you got one thing right this morning." I said. "Why don't you just start from the beginning and fill me in on your little out of season deer hunt. And don't bore me with any excuses."

"You guys each grab a sack of that deer meat and hike back to my rig up the road. Both of you will be charged with Unlawful taking of Game animal during Closed Season. From there I'll call a patrol car and they can transport you to the County Jail. It's up to you to leave your car here or have it towed. I can't assure its safety if you leave it."

"We'll leave it here and come back later." One of the poachers replied.

"Suit yourself; just remember there are guys like you two running around out here, shooting animals and sometimes cars."

"We'll take the chance; the car ain't worth shit anyway."

I radioed Dispatch and they called a patrol car with cage to come and transport the two. While waiting I took statements from both for the case report. Sgt Crager arrived and took custody of the two. "Good job Ted, I'll bet these two wish they hadn't got up early this morning. I'll photograph the meat and you can photograph the scene and we'll turn the meat over to the jail. Hell you two might even get to eat some if you stay long enough. Bon Apetit'." He laughed.

I issued the necessary citations, receipts for the meat and the rifle they used that was still back in the car. I returned to secure the car and contents, photograph and diagram the scene, then continued on my way. I was in a really good mood now. Wildlife Officers described the feeling of catching a poacher in the act as akin to shooting a trophy deer or Elk. Another feather in his cap and another tale to tell anyone who would listen.

Later in the day I spotted a couple of anglers fishing in a reservoir. Figuring them to be law abiding citizens was not in the forefront of my mind today. I watched from a distance with powerful binoculars and could see they were steadily hooking and landing some nice fish. With a five fish limit it appeared they were easily beyond that catching a fish every 5-10 minutes. None of the fish were being returned to the water so I carefully snuck within 30 yards of them. They had no idea I was around and it became obvious listening to them chatter that they had far exceeded the limit. I moved slowly in to their position and announced my presence with, "Good afternoon gentlemen, I'm Ted Arno, State Police Fish and Wildlife Officer and I would like to check licenses and your fish."

The older angler reached for his license and nervously handed it to me. The younger one pulled the stringer of Trout out of the clear water of the lakeshore and held them up for me to count.

"I only see 5 fish Gentlemen." I said. "How about the others?"

"Hey Officer, that's all we got, honest!" the older one replied.

"What's your name, sir?" I asked.

"Dean, Dean Carter, what seems to be the problem Officer?

"There really isn't any problem Dean, other than that I watched you and your friend here catch and keep at least ten fish over the last half hour or so from that little grove of trees just back there." I explained.

Dean hung his head and mumbled something under his breath about "stupid". His buddy just stood there not volunteering any information till I asked him for his license. He pulled it from his vest pocket and handed it to me.

"Well at least both of you have licenses." I commented, and then looked at the license the younger guy handed me. "What's your name?"

"Uh Deryl, yeah it's Deryl." He replied.

"Are you sure that's your name?" I asked again, looking him straight in the eye.

"Well hell yeah, can't you see, it's right there on my license. Deryl Carter."

"This license says Clifton D. Carter." I countered, never losing eye contact with the man, now looking for help from his friend.

"Damn it Willis, we just call him Deryl. His first name is Clifton but he never liked it." Dean said meekly.

"OK, who is Willis and who is Deryl?" I asked.

"Deryl is my son and Willis here didn't have a license so he borrowed Deryl's for the day. We didn't think we would run into you up here."

"Obviously!" I remarked. "Now we have exceeding the bag limit, no Angling license, Borrowing an Angling License and Loaning an angling license and Aiding in a game violation. Tell me Dean, what do you think I should do?"

"Well we didn't really mean any harm and we just wanted to get away from the old lady for a while. She doesn't like Willis much." Dean offered.

"She's probably going to like him a lot less when she finds out what this is going to cost." I replied. "I'll tell you what. I'll go easy on you two today. You get one limit of fish, Willis gets a ticket for borrowing an Angling license and Deryl gets a warning for loaning the license. You know I could write you another one for Aiding in a Game Violation but I think I know what your wife is going to do when she finds out. You're going to have all the trouble you need for one day."

"Thanks Officer. We really are sorry for what we did." Dean said.

I tossed the fish in the cooler, handed out the citation and receipt for the fish and got back in my rig. I smiled to myself just thinking about the predicaments people got themselves into trying to save a few bucks. I also felt a tinge of sympathy for the two characters leaving the lake for home. But just a little tinge!

All I looked forward to now was a big hug from my wife and kids when I got home tonight. I was one lucky guy to have a wife and kids to come home to. My first marriage was best described as a bad mistake by both of us. We were both interested in other things than making a home or having kids. We parted ways amiably and never looked back.

The Other Half of the Team

Tom Ahock was Ted's partner and one of his best friends. Tom had grown up over in the Valley west of the Cascade Mountains, the youngest of five children, whose Father was a hard working truck driver and one of the kindest men Tom ever knew. He made sure all of his kids had what they needed to get started in life even though it meant he did without most of his.

Tom made it through high school and several years of college before calling it enough for the "old man". He could see it was getting harder and harder for his Dad to pay the bills and Tom was not sure what he wanted to do with his life at 20.

He had met his love in college and nothing was going to interfere with getting married and starting a family of his own. He enlisted in the Army and the following year they were married. Tom found his niche in the military and planned to make it a career but something in his background kept gnawing at him. He devoured stories of fishing and hunting and read everything he could get his hands on about a job in fish and wildlife. It seemed like a dream at first but 8 years and three kids later it became a reality when he pulled the plug, left the military behind and began his new career with the State Police.

Tom's wife Sue knew when she married Tom that once he set his mind to doing something there was no turning back. She was pleased that he was doing what gave him the most pleasure and still provided them with a decent living. Often her friends complained that their husbands were not happy with their work, their bosses, and their humdrum lives. Tom would come home from work and fill her and their kid's time with stories and descriptions of the things he had seen.

Sue held down jobs most of the time the kids were in school. She was talented and got along with everyone. And she put up with Tom and encouraged him to follow his dreams wherever they might take him.

Throughout his life, Tom had come to many crossroads. Like the old Yogi Berra quote, "when you come to a fork in the road, take it." Tom usually never hesitated. Looking back later he would often wonder what would have happened had he taken the other path. Friends he may have never met, opportunities he may have never had, places he would have seen or not seen. It was just his way of evaluating his life.

At times Tom took Sue for granted and made bigger decisions assuming she would approve. When she didn't, sparks flew! Tom would sit and ponder while Sue either ignored him for a time or lashed out at his insensitivity. Eventually they would get over it and settle their differences as any loving couple would. Tom always loved that part. Their intensity grew over the years and Tom felt lucky listening to other men who unhappily dealt with stubborn wives and preferred to go off on their own. Tom never felt that way. When he did go hunting or fishing for a few days he missed Sue and coming home was always under the best circumstances.

Tom set out on patrol much the same way as his partner, Ted. Their areas overlapped and when circumstances called for it they teamed up to better work some of the areas. Friendly competition was a part of the job. Helping each other meant the Supervisor had little to tip favor one way or the other.

OK where did my car go?

I was told this story and the ones following by a close friend of Tom who declined to be identified. With some slight deviance the story remains in his words.

Tom would stop by a shipping company/log dump near Enterprise every few days. He would use the men working there to gather tips on game violations and suspicious activity in his patrol area. While doing so he would spend a fair amount of time in their office (a single wide trailer) eating <u>their</u> donuts and drinking <u>their</u> coffee for free. All in the name of 'pro-active' Law Enforcement, before it had a name. The men would be working or trying to work while off loading log trucks and stacking their loads in long rows.

Tom, being a jokester would 'kid around' about arresting some of them if they didn't provide him with accurate information about ongoing fish & game violators.

After a while the men working at the company decided to have their own joke on Tom. They bought a dozen fresh donuts of the kind Tom liked and brewed a fresh pot of coffee. They invited him over to get some really good information that was actually a long rambling bogus story they were all in on. At that time Tom was driving one of the old, next to be 'surveyed' patrol cars. As you know, nothing but the best of equipment for the game guys back then---right?

While he was dining on his donuts, the Front End Loader operator slipped in and picked up his patrol car. It was then carefully deposited on top of a big stack of logs. Then they waited for Tom to leave the trailer.

According to them, at first Tom was kind of calm, but didn't know what had happened to his patrol vehicle. All the men denied knowing anything and suggested Tom had left his car in a condition that allowed someone to steal it. That got Tom to start to panic, but as he began walking around looking for his car's tire tracks he spotted his patrol car sitting on an about 10'-12' long pile of logs. Then he really panickedf How did his car get up there, was there any damage and most of all just how was he going to get it down??? After enjoying Tom's predicament for a while, they relented. The Front End Loader was 'found' and his patrol car returned back to earth. According to them there was no damage done to the patrol car. According to Tom, there were a few slight dents and scrapes in the undercarriage. He immediately went out and drove through the muddiest, rock strewn road he could find, then returned the car to the patrol office with a note saying, 'for some unknown reason it didn't seem to handle quite right.' He knew OSP wasn't going to spend another dime repairing the 'junker' and it was soon taken away to be sold at one of the State auctions.

The road check

Again another story from the anonymous friend.

"I was still a Cadet back then who liked to ride around with my friend Tom when I wasn't on duty."

Tom, two other Wildlife Officers and I, set up an early season deer hunting check point far up in the woods. The site was carefully selected to be on a main logging road at a wide spot right by a small creek bridge. Approaching vehicles (from either direction) would come around a sharp curve and the road would immediately go into a steep down hill slope. The road had no shoulders and was well graveled. This meant any approaching vehicle could not stop and back up nor have somewhere to turn around until they got to the bridge.

Around the curve came this dark brown four door Rambler automobile with four men in it. They attempted to stop, but couldn't until they were about 25 yards from us. At that point we saw the sudden movements of the men in the vehicle but could not hear anything because all the windows were rolled up. Suddenly a loud **KA-FOOMP** came from the inside of the little Rambler and a hole appeared in the roof. The Rambler sat there for a few seconds when smoke began coming out the hole in the roof.

Tom motioned the car to come to our location and to roll down the driver's window. I could see the four men sitting in the car all looking pale and dazed with eyes the size of silver dollars!

Tom asked the driver to see his hunting license. The Driver took out his wallet, said he had a valid driver license and handed his driver license to Tom. The passengers just sat there staring straight ahead with this shocked expression on their faces. Tom again asked to see his hunting license, but the driver handed him his car's registration. Tom removed the guy's hunting license from his wallet and asked if he had seen or shot any deer today. The driver immediately denied they were drinking any BEER or had any BEER in the car.

At about this point it was evident everyone on the Rambler was pretty deaf and in a state of shock. Tom opened the car's rear door and removed three rifles to prevent any further accidental discharges. One of the rifles was the 30-06 that had just been fired. Keeping a straight face, Tom unloaded all the rifles and got all the ammo from everyone's pocket. He then put the rifles in the trunk and scattered in the handfuls of loose ammo.

Never once did Tom or any of us mention the newly made 'custom' hole in the car's roof, but Tom admonished them all for 'possibly' road hunting. Further warned, if we caught them again with loaded rifles driving around in the woods someone was going to go to jail. They all thanked Tom for being a nice guy and drove off. We then had a really good long laugh and joked about the experience for some time. Road hunting was tough to prove as it was and it still is legal to have loaded guns in a vehicle in Oregon.

Sign here.

Often while riding around with Tom looking for night time poachers I got to watch him in action. To this day I know of no one who could compete with the way he handled a contact. At the end of the contact many people would thank him and shake his hand for being such a nice guy, after he cited them for various violations of the law.

Finding a night time poacher driving around the back woods near La Grande who had come all the way from the valley to do their 'evil deeds', Tom would cook up a little evil of his own. Once he caught them he would manipulate the conversation around and get the poacher to agree that he was a "good hunter" who would only shoot bucks, never doe deer at night. Then Tom, convincing them he was a nice guy, would tell them he would not take their vehicles so they could continue to drive to work, etc. At that point Tom would ask them if he could write down what good hunters they were in his notebook and most everyone would agree. He would note the time of the contact in his notebook and the citation information immediately followed something along the lines of. 'My name is John Smith and I drove here from Pendleton to hunt only a buck deer (Tom would skip over the fact it wasn't deer season and the middle of the night). I would never shoot a doe deer and although I saw several tonight, I didn't shoot at any of them.' Then Tom would put a line under that and ask if it was all true, for them to sign and date. They would sign and date it, get their citation and depending on their attitude leave with or without their rifle, but pretty much always with a big "Thank You Officer."

When I watched this happen, I was amazed that anyone would sign off confirming their guilt and then shake Tom's hand for being such a kind OSP Officer! He assured me that by doing it that way he never had to worry about having to go to court on his day off. But just before I was to leave Enterprise I got a trial notice to appear on the first poacher he'd cited when I had been with him.

When I appeared at the court house, the Deputy D.A. was worrying about the fact I was a Cadet and an inexperienced witness. The defendant had hired one of the best, a Criminal Defense attorney specializing in Fish & Game cases in Oregon. That Defense Attorney bragged to the Deputy how he was going to get his client off, especially since he had a jury to work with. Remember, this was before we had to give "Discovery" to defense attorneys. So, after listening to the new Deputy D.A. 'stew' for a while, Tom brought out his notebook. It showed the defendant had signed off to the crime with my name signed as a witness. The Deputy D.A. instantly began 'expounding' on his new information and rushed out to show the Defendant and his attorney. That resulted in a very quick guilty plea.

After the guilty plea I accompanied Tom to visit with the Judge in his chambers. It seemed the Judge was quite familiar with what Tom did and very much approved of it. He chuckled talking about making that "High Priced Portland Attorney" sweat in front of his client. He fined the defendant extra for "wasting his, and the jury he had to empanel, time and trouble". The Judge indicated that he hoped I had learned something about how to be a good officer from Tom.

Take care my friend.

And I can attest that he is my friend. He had more stories to tell but some of them were a little too personal for a book like this.

CHAPTER X
The Feather

I was working out of the St. Helens office in the late 70s up in the area of Apiary Road. There were numerous logging roads spilling onto the main route between Rainier and Vernonia. I chose one at random on this rainy Sunday morning and was driving slowly along looking for anything out of the ordinary. Rounding a bend in the road I saw a dark sedan parked with the driver in the front seat. I stopped to see if anything was amiss or if he needed help.

"Nope everything is fine Officer." He said after I approached his window.

He was smoking a cigarette and listening to the car radio as I started walking back to my truck. I noticed a fresh grouse feather on the ground near his trunk, stopped and picked it up.

"Any idea where this came from?" I asked.

"No, what is it?" he replied.

"Just a grouse feather. Have you seen any around? They usually come out in the morning on gravel roads." I added.

I then asked him if he would show me the inside of his trunk so I could be sure he had not killed a Grouse. "Then I'll be on my way."

He hesitated at first then slowly unlocked the trunk and there was a freshly killed doe Deer.

"Now that doesn't look like a Grouse to me does it? I asked.

He hung his head and was silent. After some initial questions and identification, I issued him a citation for Taking Big Game Animal Closed Season, seized the deer and sent him on his way.

And incidentally I completely searched his vehicle, for the grouse, to no avail. We both concluded that a Grouse had simply lost one of its feathers in the wrong place at the wrong time. For him.

You just never knew what was around the next corner. That was what made the job so interesting.

About 8 years after retirement, I returned to work with OSP on a fulltime temporary basis in Access and Habitat, positions that were filled during hunting seasons to patrol private timberlands. I had occasion to work several interesting cases while near my old original St. Helens area.

Senior Trooper Robin May, assigned to Fish and Wildlife at St. Helens for several years contacted me regarding some information she had received of a possible illegal elk kill near Scappoose. She did not have sufficient evidence for a search warrant but decided to do a drive by of the residence in a rural area to see what we could see. The small farm and outbuildings stood clustered on a hill just off the main road. We donned camo hunting gear and used one of the old undercover vehicles so as not to draw attention. We drove by the place and could see people in the yard and in the open door of the barn.

Robin decided we could enter the premises and ask some simple questions. We went back to the office, go her marked truck and returned to the farm. Driving up the driveway we could see two people look out of the barn and then go back in. She asked me to go up to the barn while she went to the door of the house. As I started from the truck to the barn, a large dog ran out of the barn with a fresh elk leg in its mouth. On of the men in the barn tried to call the dog back but it was too late. I walked up to the open door to introduce myself and was greeted by the sight of a freshly killed elk hanging inside being butchered.

It seemed the young son had been deer hunting up the canyon and mistook the small branch bull Elk for a deer. They admitted they should have just turned it in and as I recall Robin went pretty easy on the entire case. Just some poor judgment.

Character shots

One of the most interesting complex characters I ever had occasion to converse with lived on the river and occasionally fished with a net. Other than that I knew very little about him other than the fact that he had developed a speech pattern that defied the English language. It would go something like this.

"Good morning Al, how are things going for you?"

"Yes it is a good morning as I surmise it to be inasmuch as I am incapacitated as such and I have yet to determine or surmise with any certainty whomsoever is responsible for my incapacitation as such."

We usually left shaking our heads and trying to figure out who, did what, when, where, and how.

Whenever his name came up someone usually finished the conversation with "as such".

As would be expected along the river, there were several non tribal Caucasians married to Native Americans. They were not granted tribal fishing rights but often assumed they were entitled to exercise those rights. One of them was a constant thorn in the side and persisted in getting caught fishing as a tribal member.

One night Senior Trooper Fred Patton came upon a net near Crates Point just downriver from Crates Point. We responded to assist and set up surveillance on the net. About 3:00AM we heard some voices coming from down the trail. Sure enough "Leon" was one of the small groups. We let them get into the act of pulling the net before we announced our presence. Two of the Tribal men were apprehended but Leon decided to make a break for it. He headed straight into the nastiest patch of blackberry briars on the river. 6 foot high canes were tangled together loaded with wicked thorns. Leon fought his way through the patch like a wildman, screaming and yelling all the way to the other side. We wondered whether he was alive after the screams died down and disappeared into the night.

Fred carefully picked his way into the patch of ripped and torn briars and came back with pieces of clothing that had fresh blood soaked into them.

We looked for Leon for several days then figured he had left the area for a while. Several weeks later, Fred ran into Leon in the downtown area.

He asked him if he had recovered from his sprint through the briar patch. Leon was in no mood for joking and flew into a rage. Fred went on his way, confident that Leon had paid for his crime. Leon apparently did not see the humor in it.

Elk season always brought out the worst in some people and Larry was no exception. He and his companions hunted near Friend and usually hunted both seasons although legally they could only hunt one. They were highly proficient hunters and stayed in the woods all day moving fast. Fred spotted Larry hunting and knew he did not have a second season tag. Larry spotted Fred at about the same time and the chase was on.

Bob and I assisted and surrounded the area but could not flush Larry out of the brush. The entire area was surrounded by roads and encompassed several miles. Fred and Bob however were able to spot him carrying a rifle and served him with a citation later after the season closed.

Larry went to trial and served as his own attorney, usually a mistake. We were a bit concerned that he might have a defense to the charge of Hunting with a Center fire Rifle without a Valid Elk Tag. We really could not say for certain that he was carrying a rifle and not a shotgun.

Larry however, while cross examining Bob asked him if he knew what kind of rifle he was using.

"Oh oh," we thought, "here it comes."

But Larry, when Bob answered "No' had that Aha look on his face and announced it was a 7MM Magnum and "here's the bolt! Now what do you think of that?"

Bob looked at him quizzically and answered, "I don't know, what am I supposed to think of that?"

We were sitting there awed by the bizarre turn of events. Larry was convicting himself and didn't seem to know it. The District Attorney was shaking his head in disbelief and trying to keep from laughing. The Judge just looked straight ahead.

Larry drove the final nail in when he proudly stated, "I had the bolt out and in my pocket the entire time I was hunting!"

When Larry took the stand, the District Attorney asked him if he was in fact "hunting" and carrying the rifle he so proudly spoke about. Larry went on a rambling discourse about his exploits and went so far as to talk about his cooler room where they kept the Elk they harvested. "It's a big one." he boasted. "These boys been in it several times."

The Judge had heard enough and found Larry guilty as charged.

Woody, a friend of mine for years, was riding along one night during Elk season. We were heading home after a long day in the woods and traffic was light on the Sunset Highway. I noticed a car ahead that was driving rather slow and had a difficult time keeping it in a straight line. Both of us agreed it was time to stop the car and check the driver. I was in no mood to deal with an intoxicated driver but it had to be done. There were no other patrols out on the highway that night. I activated my lights and pulled the vehicle over to the shoulder. As I walked to the driver's door the driver rolled his window down. As soon as I got a whiff of the odor I knew what was wrong. Exhaust smell poured from the car! The driver was groggy and disoriented as I opened the door and helped him into fresh air. As he recovered and began to digest the reality of how close he came to losing his life, he told me the last thing he remembered clearly was the strong odor of exhaust. The night was cold and he had rolled the window down several times but rolled it back up and continued on thinking it was not that serious and he could make it home.

We walked up and down the shoulder of the road until his head cleared, locked his car and called his wife to come and get him. He just lived a few miles down the road, but was too shaken to even try driving the rest of the way.

"Man I never thought I would be so happy to be pulled over by a State Cop!" he repeated.

"Man I never thought pulling someone over for a DUII could have such a great outcome." I replied.

What combination of timing led to us being in the right place at the right time? Those things stick in your mind long after you have forgotten other events.

On another night early in the first year of my Wildlife career, I had made it home from the third day of deer season and was relaxing with the kids. The phone rang and a strange voice asked if he could impose on me.

"Sure, what's the problem?" I asked.

"I was out hunting today up near the summit of Highway 6 and I did something I am not very proud of." He said.

"Care to tell me about it?" I asked.

"I'm a Religious man and I was out hunting by myself. I thought I saw a buck, shot once and when I went to where it was there was a doe. I panicked, gutted it and covered it up under an old log, thinking no one would ever find it." he said. "Now I feel terrible about it and I want to make it right. Could you go back up there with me and retrieve the animal?"

I'm thinking, "This is a bunch of crap! Now I have to head back out after being out all day and help some guy right his wrong." I was not happy, but I explained to my Wife and kids and headed out the door. On the way to meet him I had decided that this guy needs a wake up call.

I met the man at the local store and he got in with me. I was not in a mood for small talk so I just asked him to give me the directions. I'm sure he could tell I was miffed. We got to the road in about 45 minutes and headed up into the woods. Now the guy is unsure of where he was and I'm getting surer of what the outcome is going to be. Finally he points to a trail off the road and said he was sure that was it. I got my rope, knives and flashlight and we headed back in. Fortunately we only had to go several hundred yards when he recognized a large old blow down tree.

"That's it." He said climbing over some smaller brush and reaching under the tree. "Here it is."

I was relieved we had the animal and could head back out After we got to my truck I explained to him the necessity of being sure of your target and the fact that had he not turned in the deer and been caught he would have faced additional charges of Wanton Waste. I wasted no time writing him a citation for Unlawful Taking Doe Deer Closed Season. He said little other than "Thank you.' As we got back in the truck and headed home.

On the quiet ride home it was an especially bright night, little traffic and clear skies. I thought about all the hunters who chased deer in the woods, all the macho stories I had heard about taking a little "camp meat' or filling the freezer in July even though they were more than capable of buying the meat.

We finally got back to the store where his car was parked. He got out and started to say good night.

"Just a minute Sir, I'd like to see that copy of your citation, please?" I asked. I took the citation and tore it up, putting the remnants in my pocket. "Have a good night."

"Why did you do that?" he asked.

"Because I can and because you never made any excuses, or tried to talk your way out of it. You just looked like you really got it." I replied. "Now go out there and tell your friends that we aren't always the bad guys."

"Thanks Officer, I will and I never thought you were the bad guy."

I went home feeling really good that night.

Another time during Elk season in the Salmonberry Canyon near Fire Road 2 as I recall, I was patrolling with ODFW Biologist and we had just turned into a dead end road that had a camp at the end. I knew the people at the camp and had always pretty much counted on them to do the right thing.

We were just about in sight of the camp when a pickup broke out of a side road and turned toward the camp in front of us. They had a fresh killed elk and as soon as they saw me one of them yelled, "Linda, get your tag." The rig continued down into the camp and the several people there were laughing at Duane, Linda's husband who was with the elk. Linda came out of the camper with her tag already punched and handed it to me.

At first I'm thinking, "Ok someone killed an Elk and Linda is putting her tag on it."

Linda looked me straight in the eye and said, "Joe if you think I didn't kill that elk, you are badly mistaken. I was by myself and had no way to get it back here and I just plain forgot to leave the tag with the Elk."

The look in her eyes and the set of her jaw was enough to convince me it was a good story, if nothing else. She related how she had been left on a stand and the 5 point Bull Elk came right out in front of her. After she killed it three hunters approached her. She held her gun high and made sure they knew she was not going to give up her prize. There had been a series of incidents where Elk were taken from hunters by other groups. She was a bit rattled and headed back to camp to get help, forgetting to leave the tag with the Elk. I believed the story and made the decision to not issue the citation.

And so what! They had always kept a tight camp, and kept me advised of the goings on during the season. I owed them one.

Probably the one case that caused the most controversy occurred in the Mt. Hood Forest during the special antler less season. We were contacted by one of the Forest Service Employees who was nervous and rattled as he told us his tale. He had been hunting all day and was following a herd of cow Elk trying to get close enough for a shot. They went into a thicket and he soon got in close to them. He had not seen a Bull all day and was confident that all the Elk in the heavy brush were cows. He spotted the front half of one and pulled the trigger. To his utter dismay he had killed a 7x8 Bull Elk.

He did not hesitate after he had gutted the Elk, to come to our office to report the mishap. One of our Officers went back with him and retrieved the animal. He felt horrible about what he had done but was also fearful of the prospect of losing his job if convicted of a Class A Misdemeanor. I presented the facts to the District Attorney and asked him for his advice on how to proceed. His opinion was the man lacked any intent and the fact he had come forward and turned himself in; he had no desire to pursue the case as a criminal prosecution. However he felt the hunter should make restitution to ODFW for the loss of the trophy animal. He drew up the necessary paperwork, preventing any further criminal prosecution and set the amount of restitution at the current value of the animal. Case closed.

During our yearly in-service sessions these scenarios often came up. Wildlife Officers were split decidedly when it came to people who voluntarily turned themselves in with a mistaken animal. I personally doubt the practice of non issuance ever encouraged anyone to break the law a second time and that was the aim of Wildlife Enforcement.

Another character that comes to mind was an old Marina operator at Goble back in the 1970s. He was known as Snap or Snapper. He was always cheerful, ready to talk and loved to fish for Spring Chinook. This was the one flaw in his character although it was not a serious one. He enjoyed anchoring up behind one of the many wing dikes in the area and when he thought no one was looking he would put out and extra line. He would lay the rod on the floor letting the monofilament lay over the edge of the stern confident that non one would be able to see the third or extra line.

Often times when we were out on patrol he would call us over to his boathouse and hand a paper plate of hot fresh cooked spring Chinook over to our boat. With a wink of his eye, he would say," Caught this one on my spring line" as he referred to his extra line. He knew that we knew but had never caught him.

One day I was advised by one of his friends that Snap had developed an incurable form of cancer and did not have long to live.

Shortly after on one cold rainy spring day I was patrolling with another Trooper in the jetsled. I was operating the center console boat and the other Trooper sat with his back to the wind and his hood up trying to stay warm and dry. I saw a boat anchored ahead and headed straight for it from downriver. As we got closer I saw it was Snap and one other fisherman. I also spotted the extra line over the transom. Realizing the other Trooper did not know Snap or the condition he was in and the likelihood he would insist on writing the citation I held my hand up and made a cutting motion to Snap. The Trooper had his head down and did not realize we were coming up on the boat so paid no attention. Snap had not recognized our boat and suddenly realized what was happening. He cut the line just as we slowed up to approach the boat. The Trooper checked everything and we made some comments about the rod lying on the floor with a cut line. I winked at Snap and we left. The Trooper made mention that they were probably using three lines and I agreed they "probably" were.

Snap died a couple of weeks later and his friend called me to tell me about it. "You know one of the last things he mentioned before he died?" He asked. "He mentioned the fishing incident and smiled about how you saved him from a ticket!"

"Hell I wouldn't have given him a ticket anyway," I replied, "Maybe a warning though. He was a character!"

I've noticed recently on the little news snippets on the news page of the computer several articles about how to avoid getting cited by Police. Being courteous and honest with them is the recommended way. It has always been the recommended way. It's easy to write a ticket to a jerk.

Have you ever thrown away a Rose?

This was a true incident that happened to me in front of witnesses one night during an in-service school in Redmond, Oregon. Several of us had gone to town to have a bite to eat and were sitting at a non descript table. We noticed another table nearby had fancy table cloth, candle and wine glasses set up for what looked to be a little out of character fro this small one horse town. Naturally we inquired and the waitress told us a very wealthy Middle Eastern cattle rancher was in town to do business. Shortly his entourage arrived; with several obviously rough around the edges local ranchers and the mid eastern, dark complected man with tailored white shirt, slacks and very expensive Alligator western boots. He was definitely the center of attention and made it obvious he was a person of some means. He glanced at our table several times as if interested in us but continued his conference. Finally he got up and approached our table coming directly to me, He asked what line of work we were in and I told him. He acted as if he somehow knew that and immediately set into a pitch of sorts that led to how he wanted me to go to work for him. "Doing what?" I asked casually thinking this was some kind of joke.

"I want you to be one of my bodyguards", he replied. "I want you to travel with me wherever I go and I will pay you well."

Of course my curiosity was peaked but I wanted to assure him I was quite content with my present position. He scoffed and told me how he could offer so much more. The subject of pay and benefits arose and to him money was no object. He boasted about his 18 millions in fortune and the fact he could buy anything or anyone he wanted. I was thinking to myself, "no one buys me!"

He boldly offered $80,000 a year, all expenses paid to accompany him on his quest for more. I asked him why he needed a bodyguard so bad. His reply; "I sometimes fight with my mouth! Whatever you need, a house for your family, education for your kids. I will provide it."

By now it was getting interesting from a character standpoint and the urge to play this along to wherever it would lead. We bantered back and forth and he related his own experience about tossing a career with the Royal Saudi Air Force and going off to fly executive jet for another wealthy mid Easterner that lead to his own fortunes. Money was everything to this guy. In his estimation anyone who would turn down an offer of immediate riches was "throwing away a rose" as he would say.

I asked him what guarantee he could offer that would persuade me to leave everything and join him. He immediately countered by offering to set up a million dollar trust, in effect a contract that would be payable upon my termination for whatever reason. I can't say with certainty I wasn't sorely tempted to drop everything and run. He was adamant that I close the deal the next morning and join his organization. In case anyone wonders, he was certainly not being affected by the spirits of the bar that any of us could detect.

Naturally I declined, thanked him for his kind offer and as he stood up to leave, he looked at me and said, "You may not know this but you are throwing away a Rose that only comes along once in a lifetime."

Well it made for a great story and the rest, who knows? Ten years later I retired, made my dreams come true in Alaska and went on to many other adventures that will be the subject of my next book. What would have happened had I taken that step, if the step even existed? Only the stranger knows whether he was serious or playing games. I don't really know if I indeed tossed the Rose...

Is justice being served?

One of the more recent developments in Wildlife Enforcement that has come about is the propensity, mainly by internet outdoor sites, to label all wildlife violators as "poachers". I can look back on dozens of cases perpetrated by persons no more predisposed to break the law than the Pope. Circumstances figure into each and every case of wildlife crime and determine whether it deserves a classification of violation, misdemeanor or felony. Discussion boards online turn me off totally with their, "hang them all" mentality. Most have never witnessed or investigated a wildlife offense and assume the worst in almost every case.

I have always felt the term "poacher" was reserved for the consummate, criminally driven individual who intentionally sets out to steal, vandalize or otherwise destroy wildlife with no remorse or feeling of guilt.

I have had long discussions with respected, retired wildlife officers who feel the same way or stronger than I do. What are the reasons for case loading, exorbitant sentences and misdirected efforts toward wildlife offenses? Are we driving the hunting or fishing public, who pay the bills, away from the sport by instilling a sense of fear? Now a healthy respect and fear is not all bad, but I remember the day when our motives were to enforce the law and try to leave a violator smiling or at least with a state of mind that he had not "barely avoided a prison sentence"!

When the decoy program was instituted, for instance, it was strongly suggested to be used prudently where it was needed most. Using "legal" animals during open seasons was nearly unheard of. As the hunters became more aware of the decoy, it was felt the decoys should become more sophisticated or "robotic".

Much like highway patrol work where radar is a tool, not a solution, Officers were expected to use it when needed but also develop the ability to effectively patrol their areas. The same applies to the use of decoy animals. It has become a game of sorts, popular on reality television, popular among the audiences viewing the shows but it is not reality. Reality is long hours of sometimes unexciting work, running patrols, being visible and knowing the people in the area.

Case loading is another product of modern tactics. It is justified by the Officer because the D.A. wants it. Plea bargaining is easier when there are cases that can be disposed of. We were never permitted to charge multiple offenses unless the case required it with unrelated charges. Now a case of night hunting can bring charges of "No hunting license" "No deer tag" whatever fits.

As they used to tell us, "You don't need a hunting license to hunt at night. It's already illegal."

A while back, I got a call from Jennie Martin who was the prime mover and hostess of Ifish.net a popular fishing and hunting website. She wanted to know if she could give my phone number to Grant McComie, who hosts outdoor shows and the popular Grant's Getaways on local television stations I had known Grant for years as he used to ride along and do stories on poaching and general wildlife issues. I was eager to see what Grant had in mind. He called me and we set up an appointment to meet and talk about my previous books and poaching in general. We filmed some footage and he asked the question, "What drives people to commit large scale violations, such as illegally taking trophy animals?"

I can honestly say I did not know the real answer, whether it is greed, opportunity, thrill, criminal intent, mistake in judgment. Sometimes I feel it could be one or a combination of the latter. It is extremely hard to define when you have seen the entire gamut and realized that even good people commit what turn out to be crimes with horrendous consequences.

Several weeks later a show aired on the local news channel about a gentleman from the local area who had committed an egregious crime of harvesting a trophy Bull Elk and was swept up in an investigation that cost him hundreds of thousands of dollars in penalties, a felony record and loss of all hunting and voting privileges for life. He must spend some time talking about his crime to wildlife organizations. After the show aired with footage of me answering or trying to answer the question with Grant, my wife looked at me and asked, "What did he do?"

I wondered myself, what possible set of circumstances led to the destruction of a Trophy Elk and a human being? Have we reached the point that wildlife has become so precious, it is fitting to totally destroy the life of a human being, rather than allow them to make amends? Maybe there are those who would toss money and go on trophy killing sprees but this man did not seem like one of those. I talked about the case with a Federal Wildlife Officer I had known for years. He assured me there had to be more to the case than met the eye.

An aquaintance was charged several years ago with an undersize Sturgeon based on his own statements. He admitted he was guilty and even told the Officer how short the fish was; one inch under. The carcass was long gone and the only evidence was the filet being cooked on the campfire. He was initially charged on a Class A Misdemeanor with a fine set at $3000. His attorney was able to bargain the case to $2000 with a one year license suspension. He lost his right to a concealed carry permit due to the Class A Misdemeanor record. At about the same time, a commercial fisherman was caught with about 100 undersize Sturgeon on his boat, convicted and paid a $1000 fine but kept his license. What are we thinking?

By no means am I critical of the dedicated Wildlife Officers out there today. They are smart, well trained, well equipped and probably as capable as any that have gone before them. I only question the methods. No one can blame a well educated, trained Officer for seeking a better position but the career Wildlife Officer appears to be a thing of the past. Many others believe as I do that the selection process has passed over the guy who grew up fishing and hunting, with a wealth of knowledge about the great outdoors, wanting nothing more than to use his abilities to serve as the best Wildlife Officer he could be. The driven individuals see the position as no more than a stepping stone to something higher. I had occasion to supervise several Officers prior to retirement who readily admitted they considered Wildlife Enforcement to be nothing more than "just a job". They performed adequately and moved on.

I hope we have not lost the relationship that was so carefully built up for many years between the Wildlife Officers and the Hunter/Fishermen. Major Walt Hershey, who commanded the Wildlife Division so capably is the 1970s used to caution us to administer the law fairly and humanely and never forget that the people we were dealing with were recreating. They deserved to be left with a good impression of the Wildlife Officer.

I had occasion to read about a case recently involving several people caught gillnetting on Sauvie Island. The newspaper described it as a case of major proportion involving a number of people catching various species of fish from a lake inside the Wildlife Management Area. The nets contained more than a few

Sturgeon and the target fish Carp. For as long as I can remember ODFW has been issuing gillnet permits to individuals to control high populations of these invasive species. Whether or not a permit was issued in this case is unknown. While it may be beneficial to remove these fish from public waters it is another indiscriminate method of harvesting species that has the definite potential to kill protected species as well. The story described the discovery of the nets initially tangled and containing various game species as well as Carp. In order to make the case the nets had to be left in the water till the individuals responsible or them came back and tended them. The Troopers were able to then affect arrests but not before more fish were injured or killed.

I mentioned the fact that permits for this activity have been issued for years because in my early years prior to becoming a Wildlife Officer I had occasion to stop a pickup truck southbound on I 5 near Wilsonville in the dark early morning hours. Exposed in the open bed of the truck were several burlap bags full of fish and wet gillnets. Further inspection revealed several very nice Largemouth Bass and some undersize Sturgeon. A quick check with Wildlife Officers confirmed the fact that laws had been broken. Just like many of the cases cited in the last two books, there is little doubt violations still occur late at night under cover of darkness and often under the guise of legal fishing practice.

I don't recall the case made any headlines at the time. It was just another routine theft of State resources. The point being, with all good intentions of the managing agency, there are too many opportunities to hide behind legal activity and commit illegal acts. Wildlife Officers are spread thin enough without having to check on people operating under permits from the very agency that is sworn to manage and protect our resources. The same results emanated from issuance of far too liberal ceremonial permits in the 80s that resulted in the largest theft of fish ever recorded on the Columbia River and untold hours of enforcement time and the same thing emanates from a perfectly legal but outdated commercial gillnet fishery that, despite numerous attempts to change it by resource conscious groups continues to kill ESA and protected species fish on the Columbia River. There has to be a better way.

CHAPTER XI
The Great Gillnet War.

In my first book, "Outlaws on the Big River" I concluded the book with references to the dying gillnet industry on the Columbia River. Recent events brought this back into focus. I was fortunate to be able to get some good pictures of the old Mayger Fish Station sitting on the river just off the navigation channel and scene of many incidents of piracy against the fish. It was now abandoned but still provided a picture into the past.

In August of 2012 a passing ship generated just enough wake to topple the structure into the river and into history. It seemed an indicator of what was about to occur next.

While perfectly legal, I had never been a great fan of gillnet use in the Columbia River. Perhaps it was because of the abuse of the fishery by more than just a few and the widespread damage inflicted on all fish by the indiscriminate nets. It was a sense of entitlement and an unwillingness to change by some of the fishermen that led me to believe in and support the elimination of netting. Commercial fishing could continue without this non selective harvest method.

Around 1997, Coastal Conservation Association made itself known in the Northwest. It organization nationwide had become known for the elimination of non selective fishing practices all over the Gulf Coast and the East Coast. Most of the first members were local several generation Oregonians but soon became known as those "damn Texans" because of the fact CCA was headquartered in Texas. CCA picked its fights carefully in Oregon and Washington and went through a series of growing pains, often conflicting with other well established conservation groups. But the goal was clear, to rid the Columbia River of the indiscriminate gill nets that so often killed non target and endangered species.

The spring of 2012, Coastal Conservation Association flexed its might and gathered 147,000 signatures to put a ballot initiative before the voters to ban the use of gillnets entirely on the Columbia River. Other organizations, Northwest Steelheaders, NSIA, and Oregon Fishing Guides Association, joined forces to support the measure along with Humane Society of the United States and thousands of sport fishermen in general. Money people stepped forward with the necessary funds to pull it off.

Politicians became very uneasy at the prospect of their constituency, mainly commercial fishermen being either forced to quit or change gear in order to continue fishing. I had learned many years ago that the power of the industry usually won battles through strong unity and lots of money directed at the right places.

Sport fishermen, even though they overwhelmingly supported the idea of getting gillnets off the river simply did not and never have had the unity and perseverance that commercial fishermen had worked years to develop and strongly protect their "way of life".

Governor John Kitzhauber, a third term Governor and extremely crafty politician was working behind the scenes building a platform of his own. Few of the politicians at the State level had committed to CCA, a relative newcomer to the Oregon scene and while they courted the members, some 4000 statewide, they tended to keep a healthy distance lest they rile the commercial fishing backers. When it became apparent CCA had the numbers and the support building along with the other organizations, the gill net population became vocal and critical on the fishing chat boards. Tempers flared as long time members were disbarred from the chat boards for violating AUP procedures against personal attacks. Who could blame them? I bit my tongue more than once and treaded the threshold of be banned forever from the world of the internet chat board Ifish.net. One long time member sent me a PM urging me to tone down the rhetoric lest I go the way of others. I assured him that after 7-8 years of posting I knew just how far I could push.

With a deft political maneuver, just minutes before letters of support for the Ballot Measure 81 were due at the Secretary of State Office in Salem, parts of the strong coalition jumped ship to the Governor's counter proposal. He was offering his support to a plan that had been introduced to the legislature previously and defeated before even making it to the floor for a vote. This time, Governor Kitzhauber gave his word that he was going to do whatever it would take to remove gillnets from the mighty Columbia, the Big River.

CCA and its lone ally, HSUS were left at the door. I had submitted my letter supporting the Ballot Measure to the Secretary of State for publication in the State Voters Pamphlet and it was too late to call it back! I was fuming at first as were many others of our organization that we had been back stabbed by groups we thought had been our allies. I called the Governor's Office to try and have it removed. Nothing could be done.

Most of us were skeptical and furious with the sudden turn of events, feeling we had been sold out. A meeting of the State Board was already scheduled and a decision had to be made. Speculations were flying on the outdoor chat rooms. Members of the groups that had already run to the Governor's proposal were brassy enough to post "in your face" comments online and things were getting hot.

CCA leaders met with the Governor to try to work out a compromise. He assured them that without CCAs efforts, none of this would have ever come about and reiterated his promise to help re tool the commercial fishery on the Columbia River.

With the money support gone and the strength of the coalition gone, the fate of the ballot measure appeared to be sealed. When all the information was given to us at the State Board meeting the vote was a reluctant yes give our support to the Governor's plan. Members of CCA were now confused and justifiably angry at what they perceived to be a weakness of the leadership. Most agreed though, once they heard all the facts, that a united front was the only way deal with the issue. National CCA leaders assured us we had made the right decision. Now it was up to the States of Oregon and Washington to work out a plan for eliminating once and for all, the wasteful and antiquated gill net fishery on the Columbia River. In the meantime with non one to support it Ballot Measure 81 went down to defeat at the hands of the voters. It was foregone that without publicity or financial backing it was dead at the polls. However the commercials spent a great deal of money publicizing their plight and claimed it as a huge victory for the continued use of nets. On going meetings of both groups have taken place. There is no doubt the commercial industry feels threatened. The Governor's proposal went further than Measure 81 would have and is poised to remove all commercial fishing from the mainstem of the Columbia River. It will be an interesting outcome.

Interestingly enough the panel consisting of representatives from all the parties represented have hashed out preliminary rules, relegating gill nets to off channel areas and reserving main channel harvest for Sport Anglers. This has caused much angst and fear among the commercial community as well as the Sport community which seems to have a hard time grasping the reality of change. In the long run it appears to be the real winner in this whole scenario will be the wild runs of fish which have always been off limits but have never really been protected from incidental harvest.

Lawsuits are now pending to block the implementation of the Governor's plan. It seems incongruous that the parties that claim they make very little money from the gillnet fishery have money to spend frivolously on lawsuits.

Time will tell but 5 years ago it looked as if the status quo (gill nets) would be here for a long time to come. The following letter under the CCA heading was sent to both States in 2009 in an attempt to bring the gill net fishery into line with most other commercials fisheries reporting procedures.

It was addressed to both Wildlife Agencies and the respective Governors.

RE: Proposals for Enhancing Compliance and Law Enforcement in The Columbia River Commercial Fishery

Dear Washington and Oregon Fish & Wildlife Commissioners,

This letter is authored and endorsed by a group of retired Fish and Wildlife Officers with more than 300 years of experience combined, much of it on the Columbia River enforcing sport and commercial fishing regulations. We are speaking out in this cooperative effort in the hope that we can improve the working conditions and effectiveness of current, thinly spread enforcement officers, promote conservation, and to improve the reporting requirements for the Columbia River commercial fishery. Our proposed regulations will bring urgently needed reforms to reduce the risk of illegal gillnetting and catch reporting on the Columbia River, which affects many ESA-listed salmon and steelhead stocks, but we see no reason why the proposed reforms should not apply to Puget Sound as well.

Since the Columbia River gillnet fishery began, the Fish & Wildlife officials on both sides of the river have relied on gillnet fishermen to report their own catches of salmon and sturgeon using "fish transportation slips" The procedure assumes that fishermen will list their entire catch on these slips at the time they sell the fish to processors and they will include their total poundage as well as the number of fish caught. The glaring defect in this reporting system is that fishermen may legally possess these food fish on the water without recording their catch at all. Gillnetters have no legal requirement to report a catch until it is either sold to a buyer on the water or transported to a buyer off the river. By contrast, sport fishers must record any retained salmon, steelhead or sturgeon immediately after catching it on a tag purchased with their angling licenses.

This lack of immediate reporting requirement for commercial fishers greatly complicates law enforcement efforts. Illegal fishing must be interdicted at the point of sale, gift or other use, rather than at the time of the catch. Another aspect of the commercial fishing laws, when joined with the lax catch reporting rule, invites a serious conflict of interest. Commercial gill-netters must sell either to a wholesale dealer or to the holder of a Limited Fish Seller's Permit. The problem is that gill-netters themselves may hold both of these types of licenses. With these licenses, they may then sell fish directly to the public.

These licensing and self-reporting rules combine to create a nearly insurmountable law enforcement challenge. No simple record keeping law prevents a gillnet fisherman from retaining unrecorded fish for personal use, from transferring unrecorded fish to friends and neighbors, or from selling unrecorded fish on the black market. Over the years, law enforcement officers have attempted to interdict such practices, but the cases demand many hours of surveillance and tracking. This is due to the fact that there is no reporting rule, as with sport fishers, that would allow officers to check a catch, on the water when made, for proper recording by the fisherman.

To this complicated matrix, add the fact that gillnetting is conducted at night. For law enforcement reasons, sport fishing for sturgeon at night on the Columbia River has been prohibited for more than two decades by both Washington and Oregon. Oregon and Washington restrict angling for salmon at night in many areas of the state. The same standard should apply to the commercial fishery, which is no less difficult to enforce than the sport fisheries, if not more so. As with sport fishing, darkness compounds the enforcement challenges for the gillnet fishery and makes the important work of protecting wild salmon and steelhead stocks from over harvest or poaching even more difficult. Night fishing closures should be universal in the same areas for all users.

In the past, managers believed conflict among sport and commercial fishers justified night gillnetting. This is no longer a valid argument. The number of fishing days has decreased so dramatically for both sport and commercial fishing that there is ample time for both groups to be on the water during the daylight.

Also, fishing areas are more concentrated now, as are the fish, dispelling the argument that fishers cannot net fish as easily in the daylight. The 2008 Spring Chinook season featured a day light gillnet fishery for the bulk of the season. Quotas were easily met and enforcement officers were able to effectively monitor the fleet throughout the season.

Over the years, concerned citizens have tried to shed light on the conflicts of interest in the reporting rules and the burdens posed by night gillnetting. Unfortunately, the Commissioners and Departments have favored the flawed status quo, even while salmon and steelhead runs continue their perilous declines. They have overlooked the basic conflict inherent in a system that allows individual businessmen, *with the most to gain from subverting the system*, to have unfettered control over the timing and accuracy of their catch data reporting.

A recent case has exposed the ease with which these rules may be manipulated to understate catch numbers and essentially swindle both States out of the poundage fees and accurate harvest records they are due. After an expensive two year investigation, members of Heuker Bros., Inc. a family owned commercial and wholesale fishing business near Dodson, Oregon were found to have falsified fish catch records on over 50 occasions. They agreed to pay a $150,000 fine but will retain their licenses. They and the remainder of the fleet in Oregon and Washington may continue their gillnet fishing year after year, under the same defective regulations.

Fish catch records are used for more than just calculating poundage fees, but have a vital conservation role. Accurate records are important for monitoring quotas for various groups of fishers on the river and to protect sensitive or ESA-listed fish stocks from over harvest. Mandatory record keeping of bycatch, such as steelhead and sturgeon, is also important to provide an accurate assessment of impacts on non-target species. The Heuker brothers' disregard for the resource, coupled with their ease in falsifying records, demonstrate the inadequacy of this self-reporting system.

These commercial fishing rules must be corrected. Even in the current fiscal environment there are simple, inexpensive ways to increase compliance and ease enforcement. Reporting rules must be tightened, the conflicts of interest must be removed, and night fishing must be prohibited.

An improved rule for documentation could state as follows:

> Log books showing all catch activity while fishing shall be required. All fish must be recorded upon removing the net from the water and prior to travel or continuation of fishing (unless safety requires otherwise.) In any season where a weekly limit applies, fish must be recorded immediately upon retention by the fisher. All active fishers must carry this log book at all times while in possession of food fish. The log books shall be subject to inspection at any time by any law enforcement officer or employee of the Department of Fish and Wildlife.

A rule prohibiting night gillnetting could state as follows:

> Fishing on the main stem of the Columbia River or in SAFE areas is permitted during daylight hours only. No commercial fishing boat registered in Oregon or Washington may travel on the main stem Columbia River during the hours of darkness with fishing gear on board, except that such boats may be in transit *to or from* fishing areas. Such transit may occur no sooner than one hour prior to official daylight and no later than one hour after official sunset for the area in which the day light fishing season is set. If a fisher is unable to comply with these rules due to circumstances beyond the fisher's control, the fisher must immediately advise the United States Coast Guard of the situation on Channel 16.

Additional rules needed include:

> For each and every boat engaged in gillnetting on a particular day, fishers shall report their boat identification and license number to a Department of Fish & Wildlife hotline and report their planned fishing location by zone.

fleet in Oregon and Washington may continue their gillnet fishing year after year, under the same defective regulations.

Fish catch records are used for more than just calculating poundage fees, but have a vital conservation role. Accurate records are important for monitoring quotas for various groups of fishers on the river and to protect sensitive or ESA-listed fish stocks from over harvest. Mandatory record keeping of bycatch, such as steelhead and sturgeon, is also important to provide an accurate assessment of impacts on non-target species. The Heuker brothers' disregard for the resource, coupled with their ease in falsifying records, demonstrate the inadequacy of this self-reporting system.

These commercial fishing rules must be corrected. Even in the current fiscal environment there are simple, inexpensive ways to increase compliance and ease enforcement. Reporting rules must be tightened, the conflicts of interest must be removed, and night fishing must be prohibited.

An improved rule for documentation could state as follows:

> Log books showing all catch activity while fishing shall be required. All fish must be recorded upon removing the net from the water and prior to travel or continuation of fishing

(unless safety requires otherwise.) In any season where a weekly limit applies, fish must be recorded immediately upon retention by the fisher. All active fishers must carry this log book at all times while in possession of food fish. The log books shall be subject to inspection at any time by any law enforcement officer or employee of the Department of Fish and Wildlife.

A rule prohibiting night gillnetting could state as follows:

Fishing on the main stem of the Columbia River or in SAFE areas is permitted during daylight hours only. No commercial fishing boat registered in Oregon or Washington may travel on the main stem Columbia River during the hours of darkness with fishing gear on board, except that such boats may be in transit *to or from* fishing areas. Such transit may occur no sooner than one hour prior to official daylight and no later than one hour after official sunset for the area in which the day light fishing season is set. If a fisher is unable to comply with these rules due to circumstances beyond the fisher's control, the fisher must immediately advise the United States Coast Guard of the situation on Channel 16.

Additional rules needed include:

For each and every boat engaged in gillnetting on a particular day, fishers shall report their boat identification and license number to a Department of Fish & Wildlife hotline and report their planned fishing location by zone.

Boats engaged in the fishery should have identifying block character numbers on the hull measuring 12 inches in height and of a color contrasting with the hull.

Any undersize fish or other fish not allowed to be kept under law or the season rules shall be handled with care and safely returned to the water immediately, or handled in accordance with rules for the tangle net fishery.

These proposed regulations are long past due, and we believe that serious enforcement problems with the gillnet fishery will continue without your involvement and assistance. We hope you will consider the above regulations for implementation as soon as possible.

Sincerely,

Joe Schwab, OSP Fish & Wildlife Sgt, Ret.
CCA Oregon GRC, CRRAC

Jim Tuggle, WDFW Enforcement Sgt., Ret.
CCA Washington GRC, PSA

Ed Wickersham, USFWS Special Agent,
Ret., Chair, CCA Washington GRC

This letter was cosigned by 12 other retired Officers from both States and Federal Agencies. Unlike the myopic Agencies and Commissions the LEOs had seen the need for some kind of change.

This letter was summarily blown off as "unworkable and unnecessary" by both Agencies and the Salmon For All, the Commercial fishing group. No one expected every change to be adopted. Some change, any change may have averted the all out battle that the Sport groups, Commercial groups and Agencies of both States are engaged in now.

It appears the fish are in for a long battle. It doesn't matter who gets to kill the last wild fish. Greed, opportunity, profit. Do those words sound vaguely familiar?

CHAPTER XII
"Stuff" Game Wardens say;

"Good morning, I see you got an early start today. Funny how the sun hasn't come up yet."

"So your wife shot the first deer this morning, put her tag on it, and had to get right home so she could get the kids off to school?"

"Yes I'm sure there were antlers on that deer when you shot."

"I see, so when you arrived at the beach there was this $150 rod just sitting there in the holder and after you cast yours out, you thought you would cast it out for the owner, who has never shown up."

"So your dog ran away and you think he might be lost in the woods at night. Shining the spotlight will help him find his way home? The rifle is for scary critters, right?"

"You weren't chumming for fish; you just wanted to get rid of some old bait?"

"I see and you had just washed off your spinner and you wanted to rinse it by jerking it through the water, but this Salmon got in the way."

"Now Sir, I'm going to play you and you are going to play me. I'll tell you the story and see if you believe it."

"Stuff" People say to game wardens;

"Honest Officer, I wasn't hunting, I just had to go into the woods to take a crap and I was afraid to go without my gun"

"Well I loaned my car to my brother in law and I didn't know he put a dead deer in the trunk, honest."

"Oh the blood on my hands? I helped a kid with a bloody nose back up the road. And I don't have the key to the trunk."

"We were drifting down the Deschutes and spotted this flock of Snow Geese ahead. I got out and put the sneak on them. By the way Snow Geese don't have black wing tips do they? Why are you shaking your head?"

"You know Officer; my 10 year old was playing with my shotgun, took the plug out and forgot to put it back in. I just didn't count the shells I loaded."

"I saw this massive set of antlers in the trees and thought there was no way a Mule Deer could have a rack that big. So it's not an elk huh?"

"Dang Officer, I was waiting for legal shooting hours and heard some shots in the distance. So I figured, what the hell, it must be time to shoot."

"I can spot undercover cops every time. You see that guy over there. He looks like a cop. Not like you and me, huh?"

"Honest Officer, I know this is no bait, fly only stream. I was casting my fly and I snagged a grasshopper by accident."

Getting back together.

These and many other humorous incidents, exchanges and comments are passed around yearly at our Cow Camp Rendezvous held near Sisters in June each year. As the Hosts of the event Gary and Mary Hayden say," All purveyors of the truth are welcome!" We gather and renew old acquaintances, swap stories, sing and eat.

The first time I went to "Cow Camp" was in the early 90s before I retired. The Lieutenant asked me if I would attend to represent our District. I was eager to go and see what it was all about and hooked up the Department Travel Trailer for the trip to the area just off Century Drive southwest of Bend.

The 165 mile drive brought me to an old camp owned by Oregon Department of Fish and Wildlife along the banks of Snow Creek, a tributary of the Deschutes River. Biologists and Fish and Wildlife Officers had set up camp and were going about their business as I located a spot and set up my home for the next few days.

The rendezvous was a working session, a chance for Wildlife Officers to get together with the Biologists and see how they checked the local lakes for Trout populations and trends since the previous year. There was plenty of food and time for general discussions, poker playing and reminiscing after the day was done. The area was cleared of winter kill trees and deadfalls and the firewood cut and stacked for the 24 hour campfire.

I had tossed in my late Dad's old fly rod and reel I had given him as a gift 20 years earlier. Snow Creek was running hard nearby and full of feisty Brook Trout. We took turns with the rod catching and releasing more than a few of the Trout. The air was brisk as it was early summer and we were in the higher altitudes of Central Oregon. I was glad I brought the trailer because I had never been much in favor of sleeping in tents unless I had to.

We spent the days setting test nets in Lava Lake and a few others to see how the resident populations had wintered over. There were some huge trout in the nets the next day as well as smaller ones.

Cow Camp later evolved into a yearly gathering at the same spot. Old timers, retired and active duty, continued to come back in the summer and renew old acquaintances. Too soon it became just the retirees who came back year after year. A few of the active Troopers showed up but gradually Cow Camp aged and eventually moved to a more easily accessed location at a Campground on the Santiam Pass.

A regular group of retirees continue to make the trip each year. Motor homes, elaborate tent compounds, travel trailers and local motels are utilized. Getting together to swap old stories is never boring. The fire still burns as brightly in the souls and in the fire pit from morning until late at night when the last embers glow, stories wind down people wander off to bed and the lights go out.

It is a chance to catch up on the whereabouts and health of old friends. The stories seem to get larger and more interesting each year. The friendships get tighter as well. Email has made it so much easier to communicate but there is nothing that can match face to face exchange of information. Retired or not, if you have never been to Cow Camp, you don't know what you are missing. There is always room for another set of chairs around the fire. My wife and I cherish the friendships we have developed over the years as well as keeping in touch with the ones we had already known well.

Cow Camp

There's a place in the Pines where old guys gather
No place have they imagined to be would they rather
Here they can relive the stories of old
Here coals of campfires ward off the cold

The stories fly freely, the facts seldom matter
Who cares if it happened, it ads to the chatter.
Mark plays the guitar and sings a fine tune
While coyotes nearby howl at the moon

Their motor homes, campers and tents gather round.
They listen and engage in campfire sounds.
Of course there are the ladies who make it all go
As they listen to tales of a long time ago.

They shake their heads knowingly, humor us all
We swear it all happened just like it was told.
It's one of those moments in time that we treasure
The gamie's careers that gave so much pleasure.

The memorable moments and scenes we recall
The good we remember the bad we let fall
Memories, incidents, feats of such daring
We lived through it all and maintained our bearing

As the daylight fades on the trees in the wood
We give up our places, we'd kept if we could
Our fires grew brightly then burned into embers
The summers of life have turned into Decembers.
JRS

A typical scene at Cow Camp. "Yes, I swear it was AT LEAST THIS BIG!" L to R, Gary Hayden, Greg Anderson, Kim Reaney, and Roy Hyder.

I look back with great fondness and sometimes awe at the many experiences I shared with other Troopers. It was all part of the experience I have tried to convey through the books. I hope others who have expressed the same desire to write follow through and add to the written chronicles of Oregon Wildlife. I know there are far better writers out there than I could ever hope to be. My humble attempts have been fueled by my own satisfaction from comments of readers who continually voiced the common theme. "I never realized!"

Many thanks to all who bought the books and encouraged me to keep writing. This is my last one. Thanks to the men and women who chose to protect, and serve in a most unique and special way, and to the animals and birds, the reptiles and fish;

"Happy Trails to you!"

NOTABLE REVIEWS AND COMMENTS

International Game Warden Magazine Fall 2011 The Wardens Words by G.W. Lister

Outlaws on the Big River

"The author is a very good writer, but he is not one to excessively embellish, or mess around with a lot of superfluous detail. He provides a minimal amount of background information, then cuts right to the heart of the story, ties it all up, then moves on to the next one. As a consequence the book is very easy to read. Because it is interspersed with numerous black and white photos, the reader is easily able to conjure up the scenes in his mind, without the need for extravagant descriptions."

Outlaws in the Big Woods

"Schwab is a good storyteller and skillfully chronicles the duties of an Oregon Wildlife Officer. It's certainly not the best book I've ever read but it is quite good and better than most. Like "Big River" the author does not excessively embellish, or mess around with a lot of superfluous detail in his story telling. He provides the requisite background information, then cuts right to the heart of the story, ties it all up, then moves on to the next one. I've got no problem with that because it makes the book very readable and fresh. It is interspersed with numerous black and white photos to complement the text."

Reel Books in Review by Terry Sheely

"Good Stories personalized with first person anecdotes and reactions. I can't imagine an angler who fishes the Columbia who will not appreciate and enjoy, OUTLAWS ON THE BIG RIVER."

Northwest Sportsman February 2011
Stumptown by Terry Otto

Outlaws On The Big River

"The book is good, simple storytelling at its best. This isn't Life on the Mississippi, but the book does what Twains book did, and that is give us a window into the lives of the many people who work and play and spend their lives on the Columbia."

November 2011
Outlaws In The Big Woods

"Schwab is telling his stories through these insightful books and this second effort shows how much he has grown as a writer."

West Salem News Book Reviews by Pat Wilkins

"This book is something like an extended police report but nonetheless a gem of intriguing stories about the workings of the OSP fisheries patrols."

The Oregonian Bill Monroe OUTDOORS

"Schwab's stories are short, entertaining and as with most factual tales, far more interesting than fiction."

The book is an easy read of tales from Schwab's two-decades-plus of chasing and pinching sport and commercial lawbreakers along the Columbia River and its tributaries, from Astoria to the John Day Dam.

Amazon.com comments from readers

Thought provoking read.

The stories the author tells are not only entertaining, but brought to light the dangers and challenges that a Game Warden faces on a day to day basis.

5.0 out of 5 stars **Excellent read**, May 17, 2011
By Art Z.

This review is from: Outlaws on the Big River (Paperback)

A must read for fishing and hunting enthusiasts. Excellent stories from the career of a Oregon State Fish and Game Officer.

❖

Other books by the Author

1. Outlaws on the Big River – tales of the Authors experiences told directly as they happened.
2. Outlaws in the Big Woods –tales of the Authors experiences on the River and in the Woods of the Northwest attempting to get into the mindset of the poachers or wildlife violators.

Made in the USA
San Bernardino, CA
06 December 2014